GOING SOLO

Starting Your Own Business in Canada

GOING SOLO

Starting Your Own Business in Canada

Helene and Larry Hoffman

Toronto New York London Sydney Auckland

To Sam and Mildred Hoffman, who believed in the idea for our company and supported our freedom from the very beginning. Without their love and care we would both be still on a treadmill to nowhere.

And to Janet Rosenstock and Dennis Adair of Freelance Writing Associates, Inc. whose brilliant work, professionalism, friendship and love have made Authors' Marketing Services Ltd. and Golden Muse, its affiliate, beautiful companies with a viable future.

A Golden Muse Production

Canadian Cataloguing in Publication Data

Hoffman, Helene.
Going solo

Bibliography: p.
ISBN 0-458-96220-1

1. Self-employed—Interviews. 2. Self-employed.
3. New business enterprises. I. Hoffman, Larry.
II. Title.

HD8036.H64 650.1 C83-098418-6

Printed and bound in Canada

1 2 3 4 5 83 88 87 86 85 84

Contents

Acknowledgements

We'd like to thank all the soloists who freely gave of their time, through interviews, to help their fellow Canadians find a way to freedom through their example. The soloists interviewed for this publication deserve a standing ovation; they are Canada's future.

A company cannot exist without the help of others, so we'd like to give a special thanks to the group of experts who have worked hard to help us make Authors' Marketing Services Ltd. a success. They include: Myrna Holder and Gerry Rivera of the Bank of Commerce; Irving Rosen of Rosen, Ezrin, Ogus and Company; David Hill, Q.C., of Holmsted and Sutton; and of course all the Canadian authors with whom we've worked over the last five years.

A special thanks goes to Bill Hushion, Fred Wardle, Greg Cable, Scott Richardson and the rest of the fabulous gang at Methuen Publications.

A Personal Statement

The idea for *Going Solo: Being Your Own Boss* was conceived in February 1982 while we were watching the late news on television. On this particular day hundreds of workers had been laid off by Massey Ferguson. As men left the plant, reporters interviewed them, asking how it felt to be unemployed. Much to our amazement, grown men began to cry on prime-time TV. We asked ourselves, "Why can't these men create their own jobs through their own efforts by starting their own companies?" These plant workers seemed to be intelligent men with a lot to offer. They certainly have the same brain power as we have, and we've been going solo for almost four years.

After a trip to our accountant it became even more absurd to watch the news the following evenings. Our corporation was not as yet in the taxable earnings bracket nor were our personal incomes high enough to be taxable, yet our lifestyle was quite comfortable. We were able to do this because we had incorporated, and many of our expenses could legally be paid for by the corporation—part of our rent, travel and transportation expenses all became part of the cost of doing business. With less taxes to pay, coupled with minimal personal expenses, it seemed infinitely better to start a company.

Companies are easy to start. We registered our company in November 1978, then incorporated in February 1979 (when we found an extra $500 for our lawyer). Registering was simple; it required a trip to the local branch of the provincial Ministry of Consumer and Corporate Relations, where $2 paid for a title search to make Authors' Marketing Services our company name without infringement. Ten dollars paid for the registration, and that was it. With a notarized copy of our registration, we could sign contracts in the company name, both with publishers and authors. We could also establish a bank account. It was a revelation to discover the simplicity of the process. With our own small business, we proceeded to earn enough money to maintain the lifestyle we were used to experiencing.

Prior to going solo, we both worked for large and small corporations. With our experiences combined, we had about fifteen years in the publishing industry; quite enough to understand how to create books. Larry was the head buyer for Coles, the Book People, and Helene was promotion manager for Crown Publishers, Inc. in New York. We did not have extensive knowledge on being either agents or business people but we both soon learned by just doing the job. And that is really all a soloist does.

While our learning continued (it is still going on), we made contacts in the publishing industry wider than those we had previously, and were able to establish contact and friendships in Canada, the United States and Europe. We also learned how to write and produce books and, more importantly, how to sell manuscripts and book ideas.

Our experience as both soloists and salaried employees has qualified us to write this book. Both roles have their headaches, worries and *angst*, both have their good points. But for us, soloing is much, much better. While it's a lot easier to forget about the job when you are salaried, soloing is a way of life that provides more freedom—freedom to take advantage of all opportunities and freedom to vigorously pursue personal values. Shortly before we started our company, a free-lancing friend said, "When you compare free-lancing with life in a large corporation, the balance sheet looks equivalent; both sides are scary. It is frightening to go without knowing where the next money is coming from on the free-lance side, it is also frightening to worry about losing your job. Fright is fright is fright. There's no difference."

The money to be made soloing is based totally on the acceptance of your idea by others. You are, as owner of your business, not subject to wage control regulations in terms of your personal salary. (Your only concern is making too much money, and with a decent accountant, that problem is easily resolved.) As agents, we own a piece of everything we sell, and the pieces we own are good for the lifetime of each book. When we make a sale, it is not merely the fulfilling of a sales quota, it's money in our bank account. One good sale is better than a thousand "Good work, Jones!" from the president of a corporation.

Going solo gave us the freedom to leap onto a good idea. For example, one rainy Monday we thought up the idea for a book, *Gay Love Signs*, with a friend who became the author. We were paid handsomely for that idea. If we had been working for a publishing company, we could not have implemented the idea as quickly, nor could we have made the money we did. Once, in New York, a number of publishers were requesting a Canadian *Thorn Birds*, a stirring romantic saga of this country and its development. We returned to Toronto, sought out writers and found two fantastic free lancers, Janet Rosenstock and Dennis Adair, to work with us (and do the writing) to create a multi-volume series on Canada. So far three volumes have appeared in print, and one has made the best-sellers list. We have also sold the series to the French-language market and the publisher anticipates a potential sale of 100,000 copies for that market alone. We expect total sales to approach two million books altogether. And as agents and producers, we receive a percentage of every one of those two million. Sure beats "Good work, Jones!"

We are not particularly brilliant. Larry was trained as a historian, and Helene has a degree in sociology; no M.B.A.s here. We simply chose a different but more profitable way to earn our incomes in an industry we love.

The solo route, then, is open to all who can work, want to work, and desire the freedom to live their own lives. We can personally attest to the fact that income increases once the first three years of starting the business is over. There is no office politicking, which saves quite a bit of time. Our hours are somewhat flexible and meetings with authors occur day and night at our golden kitchen table, the birthplace of many successful ideas. Time permitting, when the weather is unbearably hot, we close up shop and go to the beach. Our business has permitted us to travel through Europe three times, and each trip paid for itself many times over through contracts made and money received. We have brainstormed book ideas in the Greek isles and on the Florida Keys. We have dined in the finest restaurants in New York,

London and Frankfurt, at the expense of publishers or governments. We have made the world our office and developed new and lasting relationships born and nurtured in the book industry.

Our colleagues are assured of a weekly paycheque, but it is hardly a guarantee of security. We are, at times, equally broke, but we retain the ability to retire at the age of forty-five because of the long-term investment value of our work. Making ends meet is the same on both sides of the fence.

We started going solo for one reason—we didn't want to be broke all our lives. We didn't want to watch our savings dwindle to nothing as we made our contribution to the inflationary spiral. We believed we were as smart as the owner of the house-cleaning service who cleaned our domain. We were as smart as the entrepreneurs of yesterday. All that they did, the Rockefellers and the Bronfmans, was take the solo route, and now their descendants command mighty corporate empires that generate billions of dollars.

We were broke when we started. Now we have some money, and our future book-earnings look quite decent. Not overwhelming but sizeable enough for us to realize our dream of a villa in southern Italy. A few more best-sellers and we'll be there. The first floor is already in place.

When we started going solo we looked back in history to the guilds, to the shoemaker on the corner, the book-binder/publisher who ran his presses in a store-front. We realized that entrepreneurship, or as we call it "going solo," is as old as mankind. Our forefathers left the farm and localized production to move to the cities and into the factories. It was an efficient mode of living for a number of years, but that time is now over. As Alvin Toffler points out, "Even as new factories are being built, the civilization that made the factory into a cathedral is dying." The trend is now back to entrepreneurship and human-sized businesses run by people.

Once you begin going solo, you will never be without a job. If one idea doesn't work, you have the freedom to try another. We made every mistake possible as a small business, yet we still survive and remain open to new ideas and new methods of making money in our profession.

Learn to go solo. Even if you end up bankrupt, you will know and understand more than you thought possible. You will learn to survive in any economy, in any way you want.

And you will be free!

Chapter 1

Everyone's a Soloist

Congratulations! Simply because you were born, you are the chairman of the Board and chief operating officer of your own company. You may consider your present assets limited, but your future growth and earning potential can transform your company into a solid blue-chip investment in a few short years.

What does all this mean? It means that since you reached the age of majority your life has been in your own hands. If you depend on a salaried job, on government unemployment benefits, or on your family, it is a dependency you created by making specific choices as you matured. It is also a dependency that can be broken by making new choices today.

It has been said that if every individual ran his or her life the way a company runs its business, wealth would come to the individual. Once you understand this concept, everything that follows is natural and simple.

The individual who views himself or herself as a company-of-one will:

- Evaluate his or her resources
- Invest his or her resources in the most profitable way possible
- Seek independence of action
- Be flexible
- Be expansive
- Seek new and better ways of increasing profit margins
- Reap the benefits of work well done

Going solo is the fine art of investing in yourself for a greater return. In this instance you can define *return* in terms of greater financial gain, greater job satisfaction, freedom of choice, and escape from the pressures created by others.

The advantages of going solo are many, the disadvantages

few. Both will be thoroughly examined in this book. But first things first: what is a soloist?

A soloist is above all an individual who takes responsibility for himself or herself. This is, in one sense, a responsibility everyone has from the beginning. But life choices place many in the position of dependency.

Who can be a soloist in the sense of career? Anyone who is willing to discard dependency and start anew.

Security

Basic security may be defined as freedom from worry about having food, clothing and shelter. But in North America security implies much more; it implies a specific lifestyle based on the rising expectations of every generation. The right or wrong of rising expectations is debatable; that most people have them is not.

If you ask people what worries them most, they answer vaguely "security." They mean that they fear they will lose the ability to provide food, clothing and shelter for their families or themselves; they fear they will not be able to give their children the same opportunities they had during the boom years; they fear they may lose all access to "little luxuries" such as eating out, going to the theatre, or travelling. The constant expression of these fears was not heard five years ago, but they are heard and heard often today. In a recent Gallup Poll, some 70 per cent of Canadians admitted they felt the country was in the midst of a major depression. They admitted to fears about their future security.

Security is the first subject the prospective soloist must consider. But he or she must learn to look at the question of security in a new and different way.

The Industrial Revolution created industries, and industries begat large corporations. In the beginning, most companies were family-owned; today, most are publicly-owned through the sale of stocks and bonds. But the controlling interest in most large corporations generally rests with a few individuals. All others involved in the corporation—the investors, the workers, the managers—supply the corporation with a needed commodity. The investors supply working capital for a return in interest; the workers supply talent and industry for a return in salary; the managers supply skill and education for a return in salary and power. But the greatest return goes to those with the controlling interest.

Through unions, labourers and white-collar workers have obtained a degree of what is looked upon as "security." Government legislation guarantees a minimum wage, a set number of vacation days and equality in hiring practices. Union contracts often include medical insurance, additional vacation time over and above that guaranteed by legislation, dental insurance, annual pay increases, cost of living increases, pregnancy leave, university education for children, low-cost loans and a plethora of other benefits.

None of these attempts to guarantee individual security to workers should be scoffed at; they were obtained through a long, difficult struggle. But do they provide security?

The answer is no. Every so-called "security" guarantee given by industry and government is dependent on employment, and employment is dependent on a fickle, constantly changing economy.

There is no one reason for the economic upheaval the world is now experiencing, but among the contributing factors are:

1. A dependency on oil that created a shortage which turned into a glut when prices forced conservation on the public. This caused billions to be spent on imported oil in the 1970s, resulting in enormous sums of money being placed in the hands of relatively few people. Those few people can now move hundreds of billions of dollars around quickly, thus destabilizing investments, gold and world-currency markets.
2. New technologies that have displaced thousands of workers.
3. Consumer goods produced in developing countries where workers have few benefits. These goods can be sold to the North American consumer for far less than the same goods manufactured in North America.
4. The enormous success of the Japanese automobile industry over the North American automobile industry. In 1970, one in every five jobs in North America was dependent on the automobile industry. The impact of failure in the automobile industry has had a ripple effect throughout the economy.

5. The disparity that exists between the developed countries and the developing countries of Asia, Africa and Latin America.

In a sense, all of these factors are interrelated, and none of them just happened. Even if the economy seems to improve, it still will be subject to wild swings—swings that are not predictable because they depend on political alliances, on the development of new technologies, even on war and peace.

Yesterday's secure employee is today's laid-off employee. Obviously, some industries are more vulnerable than others, just as some communities are more vulnerable than others. Basic industries are vulnerable to market glut; one-industry towns are vulnerable to the closure of the one industry. The point of this explanation of simplified economics is just this: traditionally defined security does not exist. If you think you have a secure position, you are incorrect. What's more, your belief makes you more vulnerable.

You are on your own; you always have been, and you always will be. Your industrial or corporate umbrella will only keep you dry until a gust of wind blows it inside out.

The soloist views security differently simply because he or she knows that it does not exist except within the individual. When you are able to see this, you are ready to go solo.

Advantages for the salaried employee:

1. You know how much you will have to spend each month.
2. You can obtain credit on the basis of your salary.
3. You know what you are going to be doing each day.
4. You know when your vacation is, and you know by law you will have at least two weeks.
5. Your taxes are taken directly out of your paycheque.
6. You may have the benefit of low-cost loans or any of the other benefits mentioned above.

Disadvantages

1. You have no control over the work you do.
2. You have no control over whether or not you will be laid off.
3. The taxes taken out of your paycheque are invested by the government at premium interest, while you are paid lower interest than you could receive at the bank.
4. All of your talent and skill goes to make others wealthy.

5. You do not have the scope to experiment except within the boundaries laid down by the firm.
6. Your vacation time, whether the guaranteed two weeks or even as much as six weeks, will usually have to be taken when it is convenient to others.
7. If you lose your job or are laid off, you may have debts to pay because you assumed your job was secure and you took on more than you could handle.
8. You can be moved from one location to another at the company's convenience.
9. You can be hired for one job and end up doing another.
10. You are subject to the pressure created by others.
11. You may be subject to office politics or favouritism.
12. You are vulnerable to personal conflicts with other employees.
13. Your position may require only a fraction of your skills.
14. You may have to commute long distances.
15. You may have to travel and be away from your family a great deal.
16. You may be the victim of a shuffle and end up tied to a job you hate.

This list could be longer because the employee has many disadvantages. But the greatest of these is the strain of fitting into someone else's mold.

The soloist is a person who simply decides to make the best deal for himself or herself. A soloist decides to take all the profits and cut out the middle man. A soloist decides to utilize all his or her talents and to develop new ones as needed.

Some soloists have never worked for anyone in their lives. Others have been fired or laid off, and many more have joyfully given up trying to fit someone else's job description. Every day more people decide to treat themselves as a company and to develop and fully use their resources.

Many soloists realized they were treating themselves badly by working for others. Many had their idea solidified by listening to fellow workers complain, while others discovered they would never obtain life's rewards working for another. Some soloists learned from their parents; seeing a father who worked fifty years for the same company suffering on a meagre pension destroyed by inflation. Others launched themselves on a lark or a dare, trying for the first time in their lives to discover how much they were really worth on the open market.

The average salaried employee has one chance in a hundred thousand of becoming president, vice-president or a member of the Board, as a reward for a lifetime of devotion to one firm. The soloist begins in that position and can benefit in terms of dollars and cents accordingly.

There are no guarantees that your own business venture will make you another Conrad Black, but your chance of making a better-than-average income is good.

Kelly LaBrash began his own company in 1967 when he retired from the Royal Canadian Mounted Police. In 1981, he sold his firm, Canadian Protection Services, for a substantial sum to the giant Argus Corporation. Argus retained Kelly LaBrash as president. He's doing the same work he did previously but now manages to play golf more frequently.

Sam Blyth began his tour operation when he was twenty-two. After five years, he is grossing millions of dollars, and he is now seriously considering a career in politics.

Michael Woods is, on the other hand, happily content earning what he describes as a "comfortable upper-middle-class income." His accounting practice also provides him with investment opportunities. A number of these investments have made him additional money, though some were disasters. But his successful investments more than cover his losses. He has made a profit by being open to all opportunities that come his way.

Len Kubas, as he approached the age of forty, resolved that he would never ask himself "what if?" He knew he had to discover whatever abilities he possessed by starting his own business. He decided to enter the field of magazine publishing and dutifully submitted his resignation to *The Toronto Star*. A short while before his resignation was to take effect, Len realized that he did not have the financial resources to begin a magazine. His employers wanted him to stay and offered to disregard the resignation. But Len had to find out if he could create and develop his own company. Kubas Research Consultants is now one of the foremost consulting firms for retailers and advertisers.

There are numerous examples of success given by the soloists we interviewed. The common thread running through their experiences is that each of them trusted their gut instincts. They looked around their communities and noted a service that was missing or a product that was needed. They filled a gap.

Michael Gowling of Michael Gowling Productions makes films for industry. He is in his element, creating jobs for himself. When Northern Telecom requires an instructional film for its employees in order to illustrate new technology, Michael is there to provide his specialized service. He writes the material, designs the story boards and creates the film. Industry needs educational video cassettes. Michael fills the need. He sees a future demand for educational films in medicine as well as in other areas. When a subject is too technical for Michael, he will hire a free-lance writer with specific knowledge. Soloists not only *have* employment, they *create* employment.

In the late 1950s, Ed Polanski believed there would be a lucrative future in cable television. Ed was in his early twenties. He had some technical training and was fresh out of school. In 1959, he went to the small town of Athabasca, Alberta (about ninety miles north of Edmonton). He presented his plan, to make cable television available to the town's residents, to the mayor, but the mayor disparaged his idea, implying he was crazy. But Ed was not discouraged, and within two weeks over 90 per cent of the town's homes were subscribing to Ed's service. Today he numbers his subscribers in the hundreds of thousands and owns twenty-five cable networks in Alberta and British Columbia. Ed describes himself as a "red-necked Western entrepreneur," and it is clear that his description is accurate.

Ed Polanski's gut instincts told him that television was here to stay and that cable television was needed to provide a wider choice to remote communities as well as to urban viewers. It didn't matter that in the 1950s people didn't know how cable television worked; what mattered was that it did work and there were no problems. Many northern Canadian communities are isolated, and television is a valuable resource for both entertainment and education. Until Ed came along, the residents of Athabasca received a weak signal beamed from Edmonton, and even when the atmospheric conditions were right, they received only the CBC. Their world of viewing was enlarged, thanks to Ed.

Opportunities for self-employment are infinite and include both products and services. Once you begin soloing, new concepts and opportunities will occur with regularity. The inventor of the Hula Hoop followed up ten years later with the Frisbee. Doubtless there were intervening years when he didn't make a dime, but because of those two inventions he is a wealthy man.

Nathan Zavier and Lynn Hubacheck, founders of Go Fer Enterprises, have made a viable business out of being flexible. If an assignment is legal, they will do it. By not restricting their activities, they have discovered they can do almost anything, whether it is planning a party, buying tickets to see *Evita*, delivering parcels or arranging secretarial services for out-of-town and in-town business people.

Nathan and Lynn often brainstorm for ideas, and they come up with some winners which pay off handsomely. Because they are free, they can take advantage of any opportunity to make money in the future. The delivery service and home-minding service they currently run can be farmed out while they work on a new concept which can turn into another money-maker.

The salaried employee can rarely take advantage of outside money-making opportunities. Moreover, as a loyal employee, ideas and inspirations belong to the firm. If they are used, a pat on the head is sufficient payment. If not, they are simply forgotten, thrown away or filed in the folder on workers' ideas that were rejected. Whether or not they would have worked is unknown, since they weren't tried. Millions of dollars in personal income potential is lost through this wasteful misdirection of energy.

When you work for someone else, you can become too concerned with the immediate to plan for the future. When you go solo, you see the world with different eyes. You are on your own, and your survival depends on your creativity and ability to make the most of all the opportunities.

Women

While this book is not specifically for women, a few words concerning women as soloists are in order because many women are in an ideal position to maximize their incomes by soloing.

There are a great many women in the work force, and the fact that in spite of high general unemployment, women are not swelling the unemployment rolls indicates that they are often underpaid and underemployed. Legislation exists to protect women employees, but it is difficult to enforce, and the statistics don't lie: the vast majority of women work for less money than men. They are hired at lower rates and fired before salary increments are due. When women are given titles and position, they are expected to fit the male mold. In a recent study cited in *Psychology Today* (September 1982) some 90 per cent of women in executive positions were over five feet seven inches, thin and wore their hair short. They were described as having "male characteristics." The study went on to suggest that shorter women with long hair were placed in low level, low-paying jobs because their looks revealed too much femininity.

In addition to what might be called "looks prejudice," women themselves undervalue their skills and sell themselves short. They accept lower salaries than men, and their salaries are heavily discounted by taxation, the cost of child-care, clothes, transportation and lunches.

As soloists, women can make maximum use of their skills. They can often work at home, thus eliminating child-care and transportation expenses. They do not have to dress as well as they might if they worked in an office, and as self-employed individuals their tax profile is radically changed by numerous deductions.

Nancy Thomson of Nancy Thomson/Investing for Women and Marlys Carruthers, Joyce Krusky and Lynn McLaughlin of Happy Cookers Publishing Ltd. are making more money than many of their sisters who re-entered the work force. Each of these women has at least forty years of living behind them, and each has a proven skill (nursing, teaching, homemaking). Their experience and their skills have been turned into well over $100,000. Ask almost any homemaker re-entering the work force how much she makes, and you can appreciate the advantages of soloing.

Eunice Webster is the mother of three teens. She quit her job to become her own boss by forming Apex Associates. Eunice earns a fair income by providing speakers to talk about success and how the average person can become successful through the realization of potential. She has a low-overhead business, and is not required to ask someone for permission to try out an idea. She makes her own decisions as the president of her own firm.

Joan Lavers of What's Cooking? is another presidential lady.

She makes her money in her own way, on her own time and is always open to money-making ideas.

Women often have unused educations and unused skills. By establishing their own businesses they can know success and the satisfaction of using dormant talent. They can set up child-care facilities, cater, offer personal shopping services, tutor, sell, open retail stores, create products and provide a multitude of other services. Women are limited only by their imaginations. There is the story of the homemaker who attended a cocktail party with her husband. At the party she met a product developer for a gigantic appliance firm. It was the day after the first Russian space flight, and the lady wryly commented that it seemed unfair that an astronaut could circle the globe in less than an hour when it took her three hours to clean her oven. Two years later, the firm the product developer worked for began to market the self-cleaning oven. The firm made millions; the lady was able only to purchase the new product. There is a message in this anecdote: women can generate million-dollar ideas, but only the soloist who values her ideas will profit. On a similar vein, there is a poem that states:

Two prisoners looked out from behind their bars;
One saw the mud, the other the stars.

Life is not a prison, but for many salaried workers their jobs can be confining and prison-like. The sky's the limit for a soloist, however, because the soloist is truly a star-seeker. The soloist often performs practical and needed services, but there are soloists who have made a fortune dealing with the amazing, the off-beat and the bizarre. The enormous variety of occupations is mindboggling. Flip through the Yellow Pages if you doubt this statement. Many companies are both humorous and creative. A recent newspaper store told of a company in California. The headline read, "Going to Heaven?" The company sent messages to the other side (heaven) via the terminally ill. The charge was $40 per message. The company received $30 and the terminally-ill patient $10. Perhaps only someone in California would think up a service like this, but it illustrates the fact that there are no parametres for the soloist—save honesty. Canadians may be more conservative than Californians, but you can Rent-a-Picket in Toronto. If your friend, lover or companion has been rotten to you, you can arrange to have him or her picketed with a sign of your choice. Fun, you bet. Clever, definitely.

Perhaps you have just spent the evening or the weekend complaining or fuming silently about your boss, your company or some pressure you have had to endure. It happens to nearly everyone. Is it worth it? The energy spent worrying about your boss or your company isn't worth a cent to you. Worrying about your own company is. Your energy should be directed toward matters that affect you and your future. Your loyalties ought to be directed toward your family and yourself, not toward your employer who has virtually no long-term interest in you. If you burn out on the job, he will not meet your expenses, visit you in the hospital or see to your family's needs. Your boss is interested in you as long as you are producing. When you are not producing you become a non-working unit within the firm's structure.

While anyone can become a soloist, there is no question that many soloists have what might be called "entrepreneurial personalities." Within the corporate-industrial structure, the entrepreneurial personality is most often found in the areas of highest pressure: sales, marketing, public relations and finance. An insurance company actuary will confirm the unhappy outlook for the average salaried entrepreneur in the above fields. There are too many ulcers at thirty, too many heart attacks at forty and far too many widows at fifty. The entrepreneur who works for himself or herself may work harder, but the same stress does not exist because the individual sets the pace. The chances of a longer, happier life are greater.

Learn a Little, Do a Lot

Michael Gowling has always treated his life as a business endeavour. When he worked for a newspaper in Hamilton, Ontario, he sold and designed ads for local businesses. Michael wasn't paid a salary by the newspaper, but he didn't mind. He wanted to learn how to design and sell advertising. Michael lived on the money he made from commissions on sales and augmented his income by charging a flat rate for ad layouts. He created his job with the newspaper by offering his selling skills and then proceeded to increase the advertising of the newspaper by helping small businesses write and design their ads, learning a tremendous amount in the process. Over the years, he utilized all of his experiences and skills. His education cost him nothing; his career is highly profitable.

Sandy Simpson of S.L. Simpson Gallery graduated from university with a B.A. in fine arts. She was advised to continue her education by taking a Master's degree. This, she was told, would enable her to find work as a researcher at the Art Gallery of Ontario. The position paid $12,000 to $15,000 a year. Sandy rejected the advice. Today Sandy is independent. She was destined to own and run her own business. She couldn't tame her ambition to wait for opportunity; she wanted to create opportunity. She opened her own art gallery, and today, at twenty-six, she is one of Canada's leading art dealers.

The dictionary defines entrepreneur as someone who is "an organizer or promoter of an activity . . . one that manages and assumes the risk of a business." Within that widely accepted context, the entrepreneur has been with us since the first harvest of grain, the buying and selling of the first house and our old favourites, the butcher, the baker and the candlestickmaker. In history, wherever there has been a dollar to be made, the entrepreneur has been there.

Certain cultural groups, notably the Armenians, Greeks, Lebanese and Jews, have practised entrepreneurship throughout the centuries. A closer look at these groups reveals that their entrepreneurial expertise was gained under duress—a duress one might well compare to the displacement of workers in today's economy.

The Jews, for example, were not allowed to own land. Thus denied, they turned elsewhere for money and that elusive security provided by money. Some became honoured physicians; a career path still followed by many. But many more became the go-betweens who brought buyers and sellers together: money lenders, pawn brokers and small retailers.

A fine example is provided by Joseph Seligman who emigrated to the United States in 1837. For a year he worked in a store owned by Asa Packer. During that year, he saved $200 from an annual salary of $400. Packer offered him a yearly raise of $100, but Seligman was anxious to go out on his own. He had noted the distance farmers had to travel to come into town to buy and sell merchandise, and he carefully catalogued what items they bought and sold. In 1838, he purchased a cart full of merchandise and set off with his pushcart through rural Pennsylvania. His theory was simple: "sell anything that can be bought cheaply, sold quickly with a little profit, small enough to place inside a pack and light enough to carry." His sons became a part of his growing business. By 1840, the Seligmans had earned enough to rent a warehouse to serve as headquarters, and later the warehouse became a store. More Seligmans were brought to America; more Seligmans became involved in the business. Twenty years after Seligman started out with his pushcart, his son's branch firm J. and W. Seligman and Company, World Bankers, helped finance the Union Army in the American Civil War. The Seligmans intermarried with the Guggenheims, the Loebs, the Strauses and the Sachs, among others. Each of the families shared two characteristics. They nearly all began with pushcarts and all ended up with untold wealth. Of course Seligman could have taken Packer's offer of a raise. Who knows? By the end of the Civil War he might have been making $1,000 a year.

Seligman belonged to the so-called age of the dinosaurs—an age when the people we now call "the Captains of Industry" were making fortunes right, left and centre. We are told that that age is over, that in order to make money today you have to have money. In short, we are told that there are no new ideas. Nonsense.

Ray Kroc made millions when he began selling franchises for McDonalds. The inventor of the Frisbee made millions too. The right idea at the right time combined with the right entrepreneur is as good as it ever was.

You can make a million as a soloist, and though this book deals primarily with those who make an above-average income, the dream is important. A soloist is one who is never quite satisfied with his or her accomplishments.

Soloist's are dreamers, but they are also intensely practical and realistic. Who had money in the past? Who will have money in the future? A soloist.

In *The Third Wave*, Alvin Toffler anticipates a time in the near future when most people will be working at home. The exorbitant cost of transportation, air pollution, wasteful fuel consumption and family needs demand home labour. Revolutionary developments in communications make work at home possible. Several banks in the United States are already experimenting with home-located clerical workers who are attached to the bank via home computers. These people do not commute to work; they communicate with their work. If Toffler is right, more of us will be moving back home to work. In such an environment, the entrepreneur is able to take advantage of the change. New services and products will be required, and the soloist will be there to provide them.

For many people, today's assembly line or repetitive job has become de-humanized. Workers are often referred to as "units of labour," and just as often, they are treated that way. Many industries recognize the de-humanizing aspects of certain jobs, but there is little that can be done to bring about change except to replace the people doing the most repetitive jobs with machines. This of course is being done, and the result is that many workers are being displaced. Displacement causes disruption and uncertainty in the economy. As the wave of the future is already upon us, we must come to recognize the advantages of soloing. Communities with dying or dead industries have to initiate co-operative survival trades and businesses. Barter, or a form of barter, may become increasingly common.

Whether the market is bullish or bearish, in the coming years tens of thousands of Canadian jobs with huge industries will simply no longer exist. How can you ask, "Is this the right time to become a soloist?"? People have always worked because work is fulfilling as well as profitable. We have to come to face the fact that security, as it is normally defined, does not exist in any economy; it exists within the individual.

Look at yourself realistically. Look at your experience, your life skills, your goals, your likes and your dislikes. Sit down and make a personal balance sheet. Are you making the right investment of your talents? Could you make a better investment by going solo in business? Remember, in reality you're already going solo. You always have been on your own.

Chapter 2
The Feeling of Going Solo

There is a vast difference between your first day on the job with Big Daddy and your first day in business for yourself. When you enter the corporate office, for example, there is someone to show you the coat closet, your office or station, and there is assistance in the matter of filling out a plethora of forms dealing with health insurance, retirement benefits and income tax. A fellow worker will tell you when the coffee break begins, what time the lunch break is, to whom you should cozy up, whom you should avoid, and from whom you should obtain supplies. If you are fortunate, someone will inform you of any difference between the company's stated policies and what it actually expects. The hours you work, the overtime pay you receive and the vacation accorded you is set minimally by the provincial government. It is quite true that many corporations offer their employees vacations and overtime pay in excess of the minimum required by law, but it is also usually true that vacation time is assigned to fit the schedule of the firm.

There are many nuances to be understood if your working career in Big Daddy's environment is to be successful. You have to learn how to circumvent red tape, office politics and generally "how to fit in." When you have grasped all the procedural essentials of your working life, you will be ready to begin making money for Big Daddy.

Conversely, when you begin going solo, the support you will receive (or not receive as the case may be) comes from friends and family. There is no one in your new business to take you by the hand and show you the ropes. Every decision, every task, is now your responsibility. But you are not alone. You may be the first person to open a Widget Boutique in Yellowknife, but you are not the first person to go solo.

The specifics of your business may be unique to your

endeavour. Nevertheless, the overall approaches and solutions to problems have been tried and tested by hundreds of thousands of soloists.

The soloists interviewed in the process of putting this book together may not have the answers to your specific problem, but you are likely to find help in their solo experiences. Collectively, they share years of experience. Mario Barocchi, owner of Art World 700, specialist in antique coins, furniture and paintings, has been in business almost twenty-five years. Ed Polanski, owner and president of QCTV in Edmonton, has been in business since 1959. Doug Dunbar has been operating College Copy Shop Ltd. since 1968.

The soloists who will share their experiences with you are not "stars," nor do they possess the keys to the kingdom of success. They are a fortunate group, not because they have guardian angels to watch over them or they have the Midas touch, but because they believe in themselves and in their ideas. They are able to maintain faith in themselves, in their intelligence and in their creations over a long period of time. Soloists have the ability to endure and to accept the highs and lows of the solo route. They have come to understand that there will be winters as well as springs; soloists accept, and have survived fluctuations in the economy. They understand their companies because they have created them and built them.

The common trait shared by the soloists interviewed was the entrepreneurial spirit. Apart from that spirit, each had different skills, educational levels, personalities and values. They varied in age, gender and ethnic background.

None of the soloists we interviewed had a Master's degree in business administration, although some had a university education or professional qualifications (usually in fields other than those in which they were actually working). It is not necessary to have an M.B.A. to run a successful business. But an M.B.A. can be useful if the business you choose to operate deals in the world of high finance. One entrepreneur, for example, took his M.B.A. and began a consultancy firm dealing with off-shore investments.

A few soloists interviewed never went past grade eight. Michael Gowling ran away from home at sixteen and never looked back. Education and earning power does not correlate with soloists.

For the most part, their knowledge comes from on-the-job training. Joan Lavers was a nurse before she opened What's Cooking?, and everything she knows about running a retail store has been learned on the job.

Soloists derive their strength from having to do the job and from wanting to do the job. The knowledge you require is as close as the salesman who walks through the door, the buyer who decides to give you a purchase order or your accountant's office.

Marlys Carruthers found that a world of people were willing to train her when she and her two associates decided to write, produce, print and sell their cookbook *Good to the Last Bite.*

The business you build makes its own demands, and in the process of meeting those demands, you learn. Eunice Webster of Apex Associates (Achievement through Personal Extension) learned how to work with hotels, find speakers that would attract a large audience and plan meetings. Michael Gowling learned how to make films for industry.

When novelists write fiction, they talk about their characters becoming real to them and how, in the process of developing the novel, the characters come to write the story. Like the novelist, the person who establishes a business has control over the medium, but the company also has a life of its own.

Running a business requires a tolerance for ambiguity. There are times when you are compelled to wait for the decisions of others. You may have to wait months for an order, then you may have to wait for the paperwork involved in contracts. You have control, but never total control. You begin to gain more control when you come to understand the rhythms of your endeavour; when you master its ups and downs. William Sutton of William J. Sutton, Special Risk Insurance, Inc. has certain times during the year when he is on the golf course because he has learned to enjoy himself and relax during slow periods. He's learned the cycle of his own business and knows exactly when times will be slack.

A successful company is based on wise decisions. All soloists make mistakes, but they also have a history of decisions well taken. The "right" decision is based on sound judgement, common sense, knowledge and self-trust. Knowledge comes to the soloist who admits a lack of understanding and sets about finding the answers. Michael Gowling has recently gone back to school to learn accounting. He wants to know as much about the world of finance as he does about the world of film. Money, he says, is like a camera; you have to know the levers to press.

After successfully launching her business, Joanna Campion gave herself a crash course in accounting. It was one thing to see a statement every quarter, but it was entirely different to have a day-to-day grasp over her credits and debits. By learning how to prepare the books, Joanna attained another level of control over her business.

Soloists achieve mastery over their lives. They are part of their creations. Hard work, persistance and faith have enabled them to succeed. Throughout the following pages you will find inspiration as well as practical advice.

Joan Lavers: I was so nervous at first. I had to take my husband with me on my initial visits to suppliers. I was afraid that I would be tongue-tied or say the wrong thing. I was terrified, scared to death.

Finally, on April 30, 1978, the store officially opened. Invitations and phone calls were sent to a number of friends to join us at an "Opening Day Celebration." All my merchandise had arrived, was priced and put on the shelves. I bought some wine and cheese, and even obtained a liquor license from the province in order to serve the wine. All the friends we invited came that night, and many of them bought something. It was a good feeling to thank them individually by name. A greater feeling came over me when strangers came into the store, had a glass of wine and then made a purchase. I didn't know who they were. I'd never met them before, and yet they were shopping in my store. At the end of the evening, I realized that I was doing it, I was running my own store.

Joanna Campion: My business is essentially a direct-mail business, so the thrill of opening the doors that many proprietors of retail businesses experience is not the same. Before we could, in effect, "open our doors" there was much to be done. The French language course had to be written first, and that took a year. In addition, advertising had to be prepared and placed in magazines and newspapers.

It was hard to be nervous or scared at the time. I was so occupied with all the other tasks of beginning the business, I didn't have any free time to be scared. There was a brief period after the course had been created and the ads placed, that I began to wonder whether anyone would respond. To make matters worse, we sent out the ads prior to one of Canada's many postal strikes. I just knew that there were positive responses waiting for me somewhere. It took almost six weeks to receive confirmation, but it was there. And I knew I was in business.

Sam Blyth: It took me close to a year and a half to launch *The Mississippi Belle.* There were thousands of minor details needing close attention, not to mention the major details. Finally it was all set up, I had everything but people to travel the river. I had a boat, I had the entertainment.

I took out an ad in *The Globe and Mail* and hoped for the best. Usually I will come into the office, when I'm in town, around ten in the morning. I couldn't sleep that night. I was in the office shortly before nine. My staff couldn't even speak to me, every phone was ringing, and people were booking space aboard *The Mississippi Belle*. It worked.

I didn't even get the opportunity to celebrate the success. I was leaving for Europe that afternoon to conduct a cross-country bicycle tour. I suspect I could have flown over to Europe that day on my own, I was feeling so good.

Chapter 3

Invest In Yourself

In the spring of 1975, Gary Dahl gave up his free time in the evenings and on weekends, and spent over $250 of his own money on an idea he had. He created the "Pet Rock." By January of 1976, Gary was on his way to becoming a millionaire.

Don Kracke went through a similar process when he created the stick-on plastic flowers which came to adorn refrigerators, notebooks, doors, walls, and about every other space that was once blank. It seemed that throughout the late 1960s and 1970s, almost everyone made use of Don Kracke's "Rickie, Tickie, Stickies."

Throughout 1980, Richard LaMotta anxiously negotiated distribution rights for his creation with a large food-processing company. He finally turned away from them, and with his own money and some funds from friends and associates, he created his own firm. Richard makes one product—the "Chipwich." In fourteen months of sales, Richard LaMotta has grossed over $30,000,000 and is licencing his chocolate-chip ice-cream sandwich in Canada, West Germany, England, Australia and Hong Kong.

Million-dollar ideas probably flit through everyone's head from time to time. To realize a comfortable profit, or even the often-dreamed-of millions, one needs the *right* idea and the firm belief that an investment in oneself will pay off handsomely.

You may not realize it, but you invest in your employer when you are employed. You believe that your employer is worthy of your investment of time, skill, talent and energy.

How much do you believe in your employer's faith in you?

- Do you have a loan against your salary?
- Do you have credit cards?
- Do you owe more than $1,000 on all your credit cards combined?
- Do you have a mortgage?

- Do you have children to educate?
- Do you expect that you will continue to have food on your table, be able to fill your car with petrol, continue to pay your rent?

If the answer to any or all of these questions is "yes," it means that consciously or unconsciously you trust and believe that your employer has faith in you and that you will continue to show your employer that you are worth the salary you receive. In addition, there is every possibility that you have insurance through your firm, that you have medical and possibly even dental coverage. Knowing you have these benefits gives you a feeling of security. But that feeling is based on one factor: *you believe your employer will continue to employ you.*

The greater your faith in your employer's faith in you, the less you plan for the future. The corporation—Big Daddy—will provide when the time comes.

And what about your investment in Big Daddy? You are willing to make this investment because Big Daddy will continue to grow, prosper and remain financially strong. But if the reverse should happen, you stand to lose.

Let us suppose that you don't work for the corporation, but that you just inherited $10,000 and are considering how to invest it.

This is the first time in your life you have ever had investment capital. If you were going to invest your precious dollars in stock in the Big Daddy Corporation, you would analyze it carefully. You would want to know its debt, its rating with Standard and Poor, Dun and Bradstreet or Dominion Bond Rating. You would want to know if it was a multi-national with home headquarters in another country (a factor that might allow it to skip the country if pressed to the wall), or if it was a trans-national firm able to shift profits from one branch plan to another whenever it was profitable to do so. You might want to know if it had heavy investments in nations that were politically unstable, or nations likely to nationalize its assets.

You would ask a multitude of questions before you invested your money, because you would be looking very closely to find out if the corporation was going to pay you dividends and, most of all, if it would be around at your retirement when you decide to cash in your chips and move to that dream villa in the south of France or that quiet rustic cottage in Haliburton. When people have money to invest they ask a lot of questions. It is seldom that they ask the same questions when they accept employment and invest their lives in a job.

One day at lunch, a friend mused over his situation. He estimated that it would cost him over $200,000 to go into business for himself. That figure was based on four years of earning power lost with his corporation, combined with the two years it would take him to reach his anticipated earning level. Unquestionably, $200,000 is an awesome amount of money for the average person, but when he analyzed his situation more closely, he conceded that at the end of six years with the corporation he would have as much money in the bank as he had that day. His personal spending would be greater (to the joy of retailers), his taxes would be heavier (to the joy of Revenue Canada), but his investment income would still be nil.

It is essential that you view your employment as an investment. It is, in fact, the biggest investment you will ever make. Given today's average salary, your lifetime earning power in a salaried job is somewhere between $900,000 and $1,800,000. That's a bigger investment that Auntie Matilda's $10,000 you recently inherited, and before you invested that $10,000, you spent months studying and looking into the future. Did you do that before you took your present job?

You can choose to invest in yourself in different ways, but ask yourself the following questions:

- Is your current job the very best investment you can make?
- Will you incur more liabilities simply because you trust the corporation for which you work?
- How dependent are you on the corporation?
- If Big Daddy gets into trouble, will you have to accept a pay cut because you have too many bills to risk losing your position?
- Are the tax advantages or disadvantages acceptable to your long-term financial picture?
- Is your financial worth increasing annually, or are you just marking time with no real increase in your standard of living or your net disposable income?

Look closely at the firm which employs you. Analyze that firm by asking the following questions. In fact, don't just ask the questions; do your best to find out the answers.

1. Will the products manufactured, or the services offered, survive difficult economic times? New technology?
2. How necessary is your job? How easily could you be replaced? (Consider technological replacement as well as personal replacement.)
3. Will the corporation be thriving in 1990? 1999?
4. Will the corporation be willing and able to pay your pension? Investigate to see how and with whom pension funds are invested. Are they in any way guaranteed?
5. How many of your co-workers are fired before they are eligible for pension or tenure?
6. Does the firm make a practice of getting rid of people as they enter higher pay-brackets and hiring newcomers who can be paid less?
7. Estimate your salary in 1990. In 1999.
8. Will your salary be high enough to live a good and comfortable life? (Estimate an annual inflation rate of at least 12 per cent.)
9. Will you still be complaining about hard work, long hours and low pay in 1990? In 1999?
10. When can you afford to retire? Can you ever afford to retire?

These are difficult but necessary questions. So-called secure jobs were never secure, and millions of workers just like you are finding this out as they discover at fifty that their incomes are decreasing rather than increasing, then look with regret at all the opportunities to make real money that passed them by. A lifetime of service and loyalty to a corporation, a small company or another individual has not led them to the elusive state of security they desired.

The owner of the firm for which you work, or its founder, was once a struggling soloist who decided to invest in himself or herself. For one reason or another the person stopped working for others and began his or her own business. The person succeeded because of hard work, perseverence and a belief in self, and is now the owner of the business that provides your job.

The owner has advantages you don't have. While you look forward to a leisurely retirement on deflated pension dollars, the owner can sell the company at a profit created by that same inflation, can use that lump sum of money to ensure a secure financial future or, if tired and in need of a break, can leave the firm in the hands of trusted employees while he or she travels around the world. If the owner dies, the company stays in the family (the same cannot be said for your job), and all revenues from company profits belong to them.

The owner cannot be laid off (although he or she may have other worries), while you can be. When your hourly or yearly rate of income increases to a point where you are just too expensive to keep, you can be phased out to be replaced by a younger person who can do your job more cheaply.

You are merely one of hundreds of investments your boss has freely made. Once you understand that you are an investment, you can discover your true worth.

In order to earn $25,000 per year, your worth to your employer, is, in reality, around $100,000 per year. The owner pays for the firm's overhead, has invested cash in equipment and often pays salaries in advance of profit. As an employee, you must pay your way by earning a sufficient amount for the company to justify your existence. In short, each employee must earn his or her salary, pay for his or her portion of the overhead, pay a share of the owner's debt servicing and contribute a share to overall profits.

Each employee's worth is evaluated in terms of the total operating cost of the corporation and the total profits. Such evaluations are not made on a truly personal level, of course; they are made by a computer which considers only the cold facts of your employment. You are a productive work unit, and funds set aside for the running of the corporation are divided among the work units. A work unit can become unprofitable or redundant. A person is laid off or replaced in the same way in which an obsolete copy machine is replaced. As soon as you begin to cost more than you contribute, you become a non-productive work unit.

Put yourself in the president's chair or in the place of the managerial staff responsible to the stockholders. How do you see yourself from this vantage point?

When you seek employment, you are searching for an

employer who is willing to invest in you. You are assessed on the basis of your resumé, your appearance and your education or specific skill. The manager of the corporation or the owner decides if you are a good investment. When you are given the job, someone has said, "Yes, we'll invest in him or her and see if our investment pays off." If you pay off, you will continue to be employed. If you don't, welcome to the unemployment line.

Other people *always* evaluate you as an investment. You should evaluate yourself in the same way. If you can be paid a $20,000 salary, what are you worth to yourself? It could be $60,000 a year within two years, and in addition you could have the freedom so cherished by soloists. Just create your own structure by building a company in which you can work and earn.

If, on the other hand, you accept the starting salary of $20,000, in three years you will likely be earning $26,000. This increase would keep you a little less than even with the inflation rate. It is worth noting that an individual earning $26,000 per year from a monthly or bi-weekly salary pays a higher percentage of income tax than the soloist making $100,000. The soloist, of course, is not eligible for unemployment insurance, paid medical insurance or other benefits the salaried worker may receive, but the benefits the soloist accords himself or herself are tax deductions.

Calculate what your salary will be in five years, ten years and fifteen years according to the normal wage increases given by your employers. Will your salary match the expected income of the successful soloist? Multiply each salary level you will achieve by four, and you will have an idea of how much money the company you work for expects you to earn within their business structure. There is a good possibility that, while working on your own, you could be worth that amount to yourself. Be certain to consider tax benefits and write-offs. Can you write off a business trip to Europe as a salaried employee? Can you write off business lunches? Can you write off one-third of your rent or the annual cost of running your house? The average salaried employee pays 30 to 50 per cent of the salary in taxes (income, property, sales tax). The average self-employed person pays less than 20 per cent of income on taxes under the present tax structure. And many sales taxes become part of deductions.

Investing in yourself is *not* difficult. The anxiety and fright you will experience at the mere thought of going solo is normal. It will pass. Anxiety leaves you as you become involved in the business of becoming a business. You must believe in yourself. You must say, "I can provide my own benefits. I can make money without Big Daddy to take care of me, and I can have my freedom of choice and work in the way I most enjoy."

Soloing is the fine art of taking full responsibility for your life and your earning power. Soloists are the founders of the businesses of tomorrow because they are the people who have the courage to believe in themselves today. There is no existing firm or corporation that was not established by a soloist—a person who decided to take the leap.

When Kelly LaBrash of Canadian Protection Services Ltd. left the Royal Canadian Mounted Police, he worked for a large American-owned detective agency. They loved him because he did his job well and made them a considerable amount of money. But Kelly realized that the only people who made money in business were the owners. That's when he decided to become a boss himself. It was that simple.

The New Economy/The Old Economy

A good friend named Jack was divisional vice-president for a large mining company. Five years ago, he was moving up the corporate ladder. His promotions were rapid, and his salary commensurate with his increased responsibilities. He was ultimately put in charge of the auto parts division of the corporation. But the wall against which the corporate ladder rested crumbled. Jack is now looking for employment in the worst job market since the Depression.

No one could accuse Jack of having made any mistakes. Like most people, he was part of a generation trained to find work within the corporation. Ten years ago, few people believed that the North American automobile industry would be in the dire straits it is in today. Since the turn of the century, the North American automobile industry had been a growing concern, with a strong union negotiating good salaries commensurate with the huge profits made by the corporations. Obviously, the good times would continue, or at least until Jack reached retirement age. This, Jack and others thought, was security. But then, that's exactly what the employees of the Indiana Buggy Whip Factory thought before a young soloist named Henry Ford came along.

No industry lasts forever. And concurrently, competition from other industrial nations and high costs compel many corporations to merge. Promises to the contrary, someone is always out of a job following a merger or takeover. Many futurists predict that the trend toward mergers and takeovers are a harbinger of tomorrow's world. Today, the "Big Three" American automobile companies have working agreements with the leading Japanese firms, and the president of General Motors believes that such agreements will be more frequent in the future. American Motors, once a thriving company, is now owned by Renault of France. And Studebaker, like the covered wagons the company once produced, has ceased to exist.

The world economy is changing. It is becoming more concentrated. But outside the giant conglomerate is the soloist who creates new economic opportunities.

Sam Bronfman's drive and vision created the Seagram's empire. Tom Watson provided the same boost to International Business Machines. One of Thomas Edison's proudest achievements was the invention of the metre, because with the installation of the metre in the home of every subscriber, Edison guaranteed payment every time one of his other inventions (the phonograph or the light bulb, to name but two) was used. Could such an invention make money today? Consider a recent joke: why hasn't solar energy been pursued as vigorously as electricity was? Because no one has figured out how to charge for the sun.

Take this joke seriously. Yes, you can spend $20,000 putting solar converters in your home. But what about a solar energy company that installs converters for $500 and charges for their use as the Hydro charges? And who will start the solar energy company? The man who invents the way to charge for the sun. That company will earn back its installation charge in twenty years by charging $1,000 a year for heat and hydro. Today, you are likely paying more than $1,000 for heat and hydro, and the hydro company is in debt to the tune of billions owing to the fact that it invested heavily in nuclear power plants. Its profits for years to come will be eaten by interest rates on those billions. Of course the hydro company doesn't have to worry. It's heavily subsidized by tax dollars and who tries to make a profit with tax dollars? But the solar energy company could be making a profit in less than twenty years if only a soloist would invent a metre that would result in its users paying for the sun.

No new ideas? Come now.

Sam Blyth is a little different from the visionaries of the past. At age twenty-two, he presented a proposal to the directors of the Shaw Festival: "Put the Festival on a train and take it on the road." To his surprise and delight, the directors accepted the idea, and the Show Train was born. Two years later, Sam chartered a riverboat, *The Mississippi Belle*, put together an excellent show and took it on the river. When interviewed, he had just returned from a three-week tour he conducted in Nepal, and was hard at work organizing a bicycle tour of China for next year. The showboat was a success. The tours are a growing success—Sam Blyth is a success.

Doug Dunbar came to Toronto via St. John, New Brunswick, with an idea but no money. Like many Maritimers, he could have chosen to walk the lonely streets of Toronto looking for a job. Not Doug. He chose to invest in himself. He worked at odd jobs at night and on weekends, but he spent his days walking the streets looking for investors. It took him three months, but he finally assembled the funds needed and College Copy Shop was born.

Walter Schroeder will never know how far he could have gone with Wood Gundy. He is too modest to say so, but he was probably the best corporate analyst they employed. For seven years, he meticulously researched and analyzed every major corporation in the country. After a year of careful planning and discussions, Schroeder believed that the time was right to invest in himself. The Canadian Bond market was booming (and still is despite the downturn in the economy); and a referee intimately familiar with the major corporations was needed. Dominion Bond Rating Service filled an important need in the Canadian financial community by providing accurate and reliable information. Today, Schroeder's service is used by financial institutions around the globe.

Andy Crosbie and Angus MacKay graduated from a course in record production at Fanshawe College. Rather than work for a major recording studio they decided to invest in themselves.

During their last year in the course, they heard a singer in a tavern in London, Ontario. After a brief conversation with the singer, they all agreed to try their luck at producing a record. The album was designated "Number One with a bullet" in the London, Ontario, market. Sales were strong in the Toronto market as well. Andy Crosbie and Angus MacKay finished their course of study and immediately invested in themselves. They created Ready Records.

The examples cited above are not unusual. Every soloist has to reach the decision to invest in himself or herself. Each fought fear and doubt, but each ultimately became confident that he or she would succeed.

Eunice Webster of Apex Associates probably speaks for all soloists when she says, "I was scared to death at first, but I had to try." All the soloists interviewed were afraid of launching out on their own, but all did. The dividends that their risk paid in the long run were compensation for any hardships encountered in the initial phase of soloing.

No one likes to worry about where their next dollar is coming from, but the soloist learns to cope. The rewards of personal freedom—of having control—make soloing worthwhile. While building a foundation for their own businesses, they changed their outlook. Today most soloists know that as long as they can run their own show, they can make a living. They experience personal growth, self-education and challenge every day. Most feel more effective.

Soloing is an investment for those without funds and for those with funds. For those with investment capital, there is no reason to work for someone else. A higher return can be had on your dollar, and certainly there is more satisfaction in the result. For those without investment capital, reaping all the rewards of your own skills is a desireable alternative to salaried employment.

The authors of this book gained a knowledge of the publishing industry when employed by others. They decided to invest in themselves and now own a portfolio of book contracts payable over the lifetime of the books which can be anywhere from one to fifty years. A contract with a large publishing firm for a book is equal to owning shares of any major corporation.

Audrey Grant of The Toronto Bridge Club employs her entire

family. There are no unemployed members of her family because Audrey invested in herself and included her family in her enterprise. Audrey's parents are retired, but they tend the desk at the door of her club and love being involved. It offers them a vastly better life than they would have in a retirement home, struggling to make ends meet and being lonely or isolated. Audrey's daughters help with the business as well. The members of the family are involved in doing the books, banking and running the business. Audrey's club is open every night of the week, with parties on all holidays. The work that has to be done is varied, and everyone gets involved. Audrey's business employs her extended family; it's a good way for families to live.

The family unit is a biological unit as well as an emotional unit. Families that work together and have a common goal are stronger for the experience. Many cultural groups retain the goal of owning and running their own family business, while the head of the nuclear family often misdirects energy and invests all his loyalties outside of himself and the family structure.

Working with others is essential; everyone gains from co-operation. But to work with others, you do not have to invest your entire life in someone else's enterprise. Satisfying and profitable work can be had, and it can involve the family unit. It is better to teach a child how to create a job and have good work habits than to allow a child to be at the mercy of others, always waiting for someone else to create opportunities.

It is predicted that the cottage industries of the future will once again include children who will learn how to manage a business from their mothers and fathers. They will learn to identify and create profitable opportunities, how to barter for essential services and how to make work more satisfying. They will learn to work with others rather than in competition with others. This is a far cry from the beginnings of the Industrial Revolution when children were sold to factories and actually lived in those factories working twelve-hour shifts on and off. The latter was brutal, exploitative child labour. But the child working with his or her own family is a part-time employee with full-time access to the family's love, affection, guidance and values.

The Industrial Revolution didn't get off to a good start in

terms of its workers. The only worker who escaped to a better life was the competitive worker who so excelled he was taken off the assembly line and put into a position as foreman. This was how a few fortunate men advanced to lower managerial positions; women and children continued to be exploited. Among male workers a psychology was born—competitive workers were rewarded, and people soon learned that the way to survive was to "ace" out their fellow workers. Laws came to prohibit child labour, to compel industry to pay minimum wages, to provide worker benefits and safety in the workplace. But the psychological climate remained. People learned to work against one another instead of with one another.

If the futurists are correct, the cottage industries of tomorrow will help change the attitude of workers, they will be less competitive and more co-operative in the workplace.

It has been said that nothing is certain save the fact that nothing will remain the same. In the last fifty years there have been remarkable changes; not the changes predicted, but nonetheless changes. Department stores you might remember have been replaced with shopping malls filled with businesses, large and small. Industries have merged into giant conglomerates. There has been a growing awareness of the finite nature of many resources; nuclear power has proven its non-violent uses to be less than anticipated; radio has given way to television; and the microchip which makes everything from tiny calculators to giant computers possible is having a dramatic impact in the workplace. Old industries die; new ones are born. Many who fear technology ought to consider that Japan—the most technologically advanced nation, the only nation to widely use robots in industry—has less unemployment than North America and Western Europe. This reality offers considerable hope. Technology makes many jobs obsolete, but it also creates new jobs. At question is not whether industries will exist in the future, it is what the quality of the workplace and the quality of life will be like. Many will choose the so-called security of employment, but this book is not for them. It is for the individual who would like an alternative; the individual who wants to create his or her own environment and his or her own quality of life.

The Dividends of Soloing

When you invest in yourself, it is natural to ask what the dividends will be. They include a certain freedom, the capacity to earn by being flexible, a choice of how much or how little time to devote to business, a choice of working hours, the opportunity to be challenged, the opportunity to educate yourself and the opportunity to be limited only by yourself.

When Doug Dunbar graduated from Cornell's hotel management program, he could have returned to Canada to join other job hunters who were selling themselves short. Instead he searched for backers and started College Copy Shop. Today he owns three stores, an interest in two others and has sufficient capital invested to allow him to have money in the future.

Toronto is richer because Sandy Simpson of S.L. Simpson Gallery contributes her skills as a fine-art major to her art gallery. Without Sandy many Canadian artists would not have had the opportunity to showcase their work and make the sales that enable them to prosper.

Sharon James of Sharon's Catering is new to soloing. She's still learning the ropes and trying new ideas. Some ideas work; some don't. Sharon finds the freedom of being on her own exhilerating; she's never had so many ideas in her life, and she is learning to concentrate her energies in order to succeed.

Walter Shroeder of Dominion Rating Service Ltd. is affluent, but recognizes that affluence isn't everything. He says, "There's only so many ways to spend it [money], only so many trips you can take, only so many dinners out. What's important to me is the work I do and the challenge of growing professionally."

The soloist is not an alienated worker far removed from the fruits of his labour. Rather, the soloist follows each and every project from start to completion, and he or she can see success in the reality of a bank account. The soloist sees his product or service in action.

Nancy Thomson of Nancy Thomson/Investing for Women experiences a sense of satisfaction when she hears the women who have taken her courses speak confidently about money with men at cocktail parties. Prior to taking the course they shied away from the subject, feeling insecure on the topic of finance. Now they join in, and they know what they are talking about. They don't stop at talking, of course; they put the knowledge they have gained to practical use by investing. By taking Nancy's course, women learn not to make the errors made by women in earlier generations. They have financial savvy, and Nancy hopes that will prevent them from living on fixed incomes, starving in later years.

No one can deny that financial rewards are life enhancing. Money enables you to broaden your horizons.

Marlys Carruthers of Happy Cookers Publishing Ltd. finds that her own earned income provides her with freedom and brings her confidence and the opportunity to be able to do what she wants to do. Marlys enjoyed purchasing two chesterfields for her living room because she didn't have to ask her husband for the money or seek his agreement. We do not all have the same desires, but Marlys' is an experience that many women envy. Women who earn for the first time in their lives or re-enter the work force after many years of being dependent all speak of the freedom their own money gives them. Marlys looks forward to the day she can walk into a travel agency and buy tickets to Hawaii for her whole family with the money she has earned herself.

Poverty, on the other hand, is debilitating, constricting, anxiety-producing and limiting. With little opportunity for enrichment and no control over one's destiny, it is easy to be captive to the survival syndrome.

Fred Bird's success as a photographer has enabled him to go South at every available opportunity. Besides being Canada's foremost food photographer, he excels in travel photos. Every winter, Fred goes South for several weeks on assignment. Each trip is no more than a week or two, but each trip allows Fred to revitalize himself and escape the harsh winter. As a bonus, Fred is paid to go to the Caribbean.

A recent television talk-show featured interviews with several young entrepreneurs who spoke with excitement about their new enterprises. The audience frowned on them, accusing them of "only being in business for the money." This is a typical attitude. It is all right for a person to be employed and earning because we have been brainwashed to believe that only salaried employment is honourable. Of course the firm that employs these honourable workers is in business to make money, but the audience failed to recognize this fact, just as it failed to realize that the soloists were creating businesses that would also employ honourable workers like themselves. There is nothing unsavory about making money, assuming it is made legally and without exploitation of others. People who do not make money cannot pay salaries or buy consumer products. Without the purchase of consumer products, the economy goes bust.

But consider the audience; these are the same people who will complain that their salaries are too low, that they do not receive adequate benefits and that everything is too expensive. They suffer from the misconception that money earned in someone else's employ is somehow different from the money earned in one's own business.

But making money is only part of it. Businesses are creations of the mind, and the owners of these businesses have a right to be proud. Those with employees contribute jobs and products or services. They fill a need in their communities.

Laurie Greenwood of Greenwood's Books is twenty-two and is doing well as co-principal in the bookstore she owns with her siblings. Her on-the-job management program is providing Laurie with the best education she could have.

While some others struggle through their M.B.A. programs, learning the nuances of big biz, Laurie has direct experience. If she chooses to invest in a book by putting it into her store, she is taking a risk. If the book sells, she makes a profit; if it does not, she learns from her mistake. Laurie will learn to move books, to keep inventories, to finance, and she will learn public relations because she deals with the public. Laurie will have a business education far more valuable than many who spend thousands of dollars on higher education.

Much career counselling in schools and a good deal of preparatory education is aimed at helping students find positions in the existing business structure. Courses that encourage entrepreneurs are relatively new. While young people in the Silicon Valley in California are becoming millionaires by starting their own computer or computer-related businesses, many Canadian children are sitting in classrooms learning how to fill existing jobs. Their exposure to computers is a course in how to use them. Canada has a terrible record in the matter of providing R&D Funds (Research and Development). If this short-sightedness is not redressed, ground that has been gained will be lost, and we will remain the hewers of wood and the drawers of water.

Training for existing jobs is not entirely to be condemned, of course. But it must be asked just how many people IBM, Dome Petroleum, Canadian Tire and other large firms will require in the future.

The graduating university student is skilled and has talent and ideas. He or she is alive with enthusiasm. Sadly, many are also unemployed and thrust into a job market with little opportunity. This fact raises serious questions about the educational system and the type of education our children are receiving. These same students, with encouragement, could be creating businesses that provide employment. If our most talented and our best-trained young people don't invest in themselves, who will?

A career, in the broadest sense of the word, is an investment of time, energy, creativity, skills and imagination. It is up to you to decide where you want to invest. An investment in yourself can pay big dividends. Go solo.

Chapter 4
Marketing Your Skills

Whether you are a nurse, a homemaker, or a worker for the Post Office, the chances are you already know something about business. You realize the value of dependability, thrift and efficiency. You know that others need you, and you know your success is based on your performance.

When you work for Big Daddy, all that is required is a portion of your total life skills. For example, Mary in the accounting department is only called upon to enter figures in the books. Mary may have a talent for bringing in new business to increase those figures, but bringing in new business is not her job. Ted is one of Big Daddy's top salesmen. Month after month, Ted writes up as many orders as half the entire department. Occasionally, the people in the product development division will ask for Ted's opinion on a new item. But they do so only to confirm their own beliefs. They've read all the translations of Japanese business books, and they seek the consensus so prized by Japanese firms. They have yet to ask Ted what he would like to sell or what he thinks would sell. Ted has been selling a long while, and he has direct access to the market. The chances are that Ted has some fine innovative ideas, but that's not his department.

Large companies put their employees in neat niches: typists do not write letters; file clerks do not use word processors; salesmen do not initiate product lines; product developers do not sell; executive secretaries do not do accounting; accountants do not file; ad nauseam. Admittedly, the smaller the company for which you work, the greater your chance of using more of your skills.

When you work for yourself every skill you have acquired in your life is utilized, and new ones are mastered. You'll be surprised at the variety and extent of the skills you already possess. Once you fully recognize those skills and look at the requirements for going solo, you'll discover that you have, at worst, a handful of missing skills. These missing skills can be developed.

Building on your existing skills is what going solo is all about. Marlys Carruthers, a former nurse, decided one day to write and market a cookbook with two of her friends in Calgary. Since all of them were good cooks, they decided to call their cookbook *Good to the Last Bite*. All three women were new to publishing and business. They had to work from scratch and learn as they involved themselves. Writing a book is one task; publishing and distributing involves entry into a complex world where large publishing firms and distribution agencies control the market place. Marlys and her friends had varied skills: nursing, homemaking (and all that goes with homemaking) and, of course, cooking. They had children at home as well. The women did, however, possess excellent organizing talents and an ability to get the job done. Their enthusiasm for the project brought them a best-seller (38,000 copies so far), and a considerable profit. Basic skills combined with hard work and willingness to learn resulted in their success.

Nancy Thomson of Nancy Thomson/Investing for Women was a homemaker and teacher prior to her studies of investment strategies. Extensive reading and classroom instruction provided Nancy with inspiration. She created an eight-week course for women on how to invest.

Faith in yourself and your earning power is a matter of understanding how much your skills are worth. For example, Andrew Crosbie and Angus MacKay learned how to make phonograph records at Fanshawe College when they were twenty. They, like other students, could have taken their skill and found employment with an existing record company. Andrew and Angus had families with spare cash to invest, a thousand here and a thousand there. They created a record using a local rock group. Andrew and Angus started small, planning on a record that would help them make a profit to enable them to repay their families. They didn't expect to make enough money to start Ready Records, but they did. By doing what they wanted—actually making their own record—they learned a great deal about the recording industry and found their own place as independents in a competitive field.

Doug Dunbar was a graduate student in hotel management

when he managed a copy shop to earn extra money. He was such a fine manager that the company asked him to open a new location using their label. Instead, Doug Dunbar realized he had the skill to open his own shop. He found people who were willing to invest in his idea. Doug Dunbar was penniless when he started in 1968, but if you ask him today about his finances, you will receive a wide smile. Trained in one skill, it was his part-time job that ended up becoming his career. He now owns several copy shops, and who knows, one day he might put his other skills to work and buy his own hotel to manage.

Soloists generally start small. Their spare room or basement offices do not initially speak of success, but as they work they do use every skill they have acquired, and they do learn new ones.

In the halls of higher education, Janet Rosenstock of Freelance Writing Associates, Inc. was a fine literary student and a mediocre math student. But now, without hesitation, she can tell you how much interest she loses on unpaid accounts, how much interest she will make on funds invested, what tax shelters are available, what investments in equipment qualify for tax rebates and how much the royalties will be on any one book. And she has mastered the mysteries of double entry accounting. She says, "I used to sleep through math, but when it was my money I learned how to invest it, how to keep good books, and how to make it all balance. What I used to find boring is now a matter of fascination."

You are more skilled than you think. A secretary is highly trained, and usually he or she has a variety of skills. Lynn Hubacheck used to be a secretary before she and Nathan Zavier founded Go Fer Enterprises. For $10 per hour, this company will type for out-of-town business men in their hotel or Lynn may organize and plan a party for the sales force of a major corporation. Lynn is using all her skills as a secretary in her own enterprise, and adding more skills as she strives to cope with the demands of her varied business. Today she is enrolled in an accounting course because she wants to know more about finance and how to keep her own books. Everything Lynn learned as a secretary is paying off for her.

Michael Gowling started building his valuable skills when he was twelve and first held a movie camera. He went around the neighbourhood filming incidents and landscapes, and soon his know-how increased. In the meantime, he rented films to show in his neighbourhood. At thirty-four, Michael's skills as a film producer are valuable, and he knows it. He has managed to develop himself fully, and he makes money.

Analyze your own experiences and the skills you have acquired through those experiences. Include the slightest bits of information even if you feel they are insignificant. Keep a running list and add to it over several weeks. Do not forget to add skills you acquired doing volunteer work or as a result of some hobby.

Here are some of the items that might appear:

> typing; writing; researching; management; cooking; cleaning; driving; designing; organizing; reading; repairing appliances, furniture, rooves, garage doors or any other speciality; upholstering; accounting/bookkeeping; child-care.

Your list might contain many skills not mentioned. Just to give you an idea of what can be done with simple skills—skills everyone takes for granted—here are a few examples.

One young person who had considerable experience baby-sitting also enjoyed reading aloud. She organized a story-time for neighbourhood kids and charged parents a baby-sitting fee for each of the fifteen youngsters. She read to them and helped the children act out the stories. The parents sent their children to her for two-hour sessions (held twice a week) and used the time to do their shopping.

One woman who was bedridden offered a greeting card service. From her home, she charged her customers by the card. She wrote, addressed and stamped Christmas cards, New Year's cards and eventually expanded into form letters for several small businesses who wanted to communicate with their customers in a more personal way.

These are only two examples, but they illustrate the fact that a soloist can make money utilizing both simple and complex skills. When asked what skills he possessed, *Siddhartha*, the hero of the novel by the same name, replied, "I can think, I can fast, I can wait." Those may be all the skills you need in order to go solo. But any and all of your abilities can have a direct application.

To go solo, you will either have or acquire the following skills:

1. *The Ability to Sell*
Whatever business you choose to enter, somebody is required to purchase your product or service. You must learn to sell and to make prospective purchasers aware of the product you offer or the service you render.

All that is required is the ability to communicate clearly and a product or service that fills a need. Joanna Campion, founder of Campion Language Studies, was frightened when she went out on her first sales call, but she discovered that her product was valuable. The best salesmen do not always make the most sales; that accolade generally goes to the salesperson selling the best product or service.

2. *Bookkeeping and an Understanding of Finance*
If you can balance your cheque book you are well on the road to financial savvy. The art of bookkeeping is slightly more refined than keeping a cheque book, but essentially the technique is identical. Everything you do costs money. Few people are in the position of Citizen Kane who, in the film dialogue, was told that one of his companies was losing a million dollars a year. He retorted, "At that rate, I'll be broke in fifty years!" Yes, *Citizen Kane* is a film; a fantasy. As a beginning soloist you can't afford to lose fifty cents. You have to learn to keep your books.

3. *Financing*
It is always said that you must have money to make money. This is a myth. It takes money to make money if only the money is going to work. If *you* work, you do not necessarily need a starting fund. Certainly, it helps to have money when you are going solo, but financing can be acquired through your own efforts. If you can sell your product or services to ordinary people, you can sell the idea to the bank. There are funds to be had if you can illustrate how your product or service will succeed.

When you approach a banker, or an external financial source, you will have to prepare a proposal, and it is wise to consult a professional accountant first. The proposal is simply a statement made in dollars and cents and concerns the potential earning power of your product or service in the coming years. Essentially, you are asking to borrow money and explaining how and when the money will be paid back. If you have ever taken out a loan for anything, you have probably been through this process before.

4. *Advertising and Public Relations*

Every child who has ever opened up a lemonade stand knows something about advertising. First the child writes L-E-M-O-N-A-D-E on the front of the stand, including the price. Then he or she does the same on a piece of paper, making a few copies. The youngster posts these on trees and telephone poles. When you start going solo, the principles applied are the same as those applied by the youngster selling lemonade.

Define your product or service. List the price. And see to it that the information reaches prospective customers. Brad, Gail and Laurie Greenwood of Edmonton have been successful for the past three years. They knew how to keep books and inventory records and that was part of the reason they opened their own bookstore. They knew little about advertising, but they were willing to learn. They asked where to place advertising, and they inquired about just what information should go into the ad. Their friends were eager to help. At first their approach was trial and error. Certain ads worked better than others, and certain vehicles for their advertising pulled in more customers than others. But within a year, their "lemonade" signs were working.

5. *The Ability to Do a Good Job*

The ability to do a good job grows out of doing it—and doing it wholeheartedly. This is made much easier by the fact that the enterprise is totally yours and will at every phase of operation reflect your strength and dedication. Doug Dunbar calls it "commitment." And commitment is the mainstay of every soloist's business. When a customer drops off materials to be copied at Doug's College Copy Shop and asks for the copies the next morning, Doug sees that they are ready. Even if his staff has to work overtime, Doug has a commitment to his customers and meets his deadlines. Meeting deadlines is extremely important to the soloist. Bell Telephone may tell you that a repair man will come at three p.m. to repair your telephone and will not come till five. The repair man will just smile and mumble, "We were busier than expected," or "We can't make specific commitments." You have to accept it because Bell has a monopoly. Where are you going to get another phone company?

The soloist can't afford this kind of behaviour. Deliveries must be made on time; services must be performed when they are contracted. A soloist is made or broken by his attitude toward deadlines.

6. *Confidence and Enthusiasm*

These attitudes are essential for the soloist who wants to succeed. When William Sutton started going solo, the first obstacle he had to overcome was worry. Worry is a luxury which belongs to middle management within the corporation. A soloist has too much to do to spend time worrying. For Sutton, the cure for his worry was "to work like hell eight hours a day." Many soloists work longer hours than salaried employees; but the key factor is that they are working for themselves, and they enjoy what they are doing.

Confidence is gained with success, and enthusiasm grows as you realize your product or service is selling. Walter Schroeder constantly maintains that his service is the *best* in the business. He has faith in his ability to analyze the bond market, and the continued and expanded use of his service has proved him right.

7. *Collecting*

You own a hotel on Boardwalk and one of your opponents lands there. You want $2,000 for rent immediately; you do not want to wait thirty, sixty or ninety days. One month's interest on $2,000 at current rates is $20. The $2,000 should be in your bank account earning interest, not in the bank account of the person who has already made use of your service or who has taken delivery of your product. You do not want to wait for someone else to be in a liquid position. Even your children want their allowances when due. Collecting what is owed you becomes easier as you gain experience. It is a skill you develop because it grows out of need.

When Fred Bird started going solo, it took him literally hours to gain the courage to become a bill collector. He had little choice. He had bills of his own to pay, a payroll to meet and food to put on his table. Generally the amount Fred was owed was little more than a day's interest for the owing firm. Fred realized that it was his money the other company was holding; he quickly overcame his fear of asking for what was his. There is more on the art of collecting later in this book.

8. *Discipline*
A novice teacher soon discovers that the child she appoints to take charge of the class while she runs to the office for a minute is stricter than she is. Suddenly, the child is no longer the one being disciplined but is elevated to the role of disciplinarian. *Self-discipline* comes easily to the soloist: it's a matter of survival. Soloists Janet Rosenstock and Dennis Adair of Freelance Writing Associates, Inc. worked eight to nine hours a day, seven days a week and some evenings for three years when they initiated their business. During the first three years they never took a vacation or had a holiday off. Because of the high-risk nature of their business, they never turned down any assignment. Their self-discipline was directly related to their survival instincts. No corporation would have allowed employees to work such hours, but when you are working for yourself, everything changes.

9. *Perseverence*
Few soloists take off like a rocket. There are day-to-day ups and downs; there is happiness and misery; there are realized expectations and failed dreams. And sometimes there is a lot of sitting by the phone and waiting for it to ring. The ability to persevere sees you through the worst of times; it is reinforced each time you know success. You must have belief in yourself in order to have staying power.

Andrew Crosbie recently returned from California where he firmed up an agreement for distribution of his phonograph record lines in the United States. This arrangement can be worth millions to him, but Andrew would be the first to concede that his success did not come overnight. It has taken over four years—of brown-bag lunches, spaghetti for dinner, no vacations and, at times, the ability to keep one step ahead of his creditors—to succeed. Andrew and his partner Angus never doubted the result; they willingly persevered through it all to see their hopes and dreams come to fruition.

The skills needed to be a successful soloist are neither mystical nor beyond reach. The soloist utilizes knowledge, learning ability and experience and combines these with faith in himself.

Going solo is the act of permitting yourself to be a whole person; to use all of yourself and your acquired skills and knowledge to make a living by doing what you enjoy.

Many soloists are pleasantly surprised at how readily the business community accepts and encourages them. In fact, many firms prefer soloists to full-time staff. Doug Dunbar noted how many companies who owned their own copying equipment and had trained operators sent him the larger jobs. They simply found it more economical to send material to Doug than tie up their machine and operator for an extended period.

The owners of a large office building find it more efficient and less expensive to hire Kelly LaBrash's security service than hire their own security staff. Kelly guarantees the professionalism of his employees, and at the same time it is he who incurs the mountain of paperwork that accompanies the maintenace of a large staff.

When you market your skills to the fullest, you are no longer compelled to accept any job. You create your own. Whatever you choose to do can be done as a free lancer. If you have a flair for knitting or you own a loom, you can make clothes and sweaters. You can sell them through local service clubs, by mail order or to local shops. You may eventually hire additional staff to create more clothing. You may not become another Wabassco, but it is likely that you will earn a reasonable income based on your own skills and by doing what you excel at.

Sharon James has acquired a sizeable reputation in her community as an excellent cook. If she agreed to bring a dish, she was guaranteed an invitation; her hosts provided the remainder of the food and the liquid refreshment. By 1980, Sharon's friends were asking her to cater some of their parties. Her dishes maintained their previous high quality, and each party she catered led to another request. Sharon won't put Cara or VersaFood out of business, but within her area of downtown Toronto, Sharon's Catering Service is firmly entrenched. Her skill as a cook, combined with her organizational ability, has made her company a success.

Charlotte Fielden has been a novelist, a playwright, a teacher and minister. She acknowledges her skills and knows what makes her happiest. She's open to new experiences and does what she wants. The work she enjoys and the variety in her life comes to her simply through the act of being available and seeking out the wealth of opportunities open to her. Charlotte has always lived frugally, and her determination not to waste money has enabled her to travel the world extensively, seeking new experiences and opportunities. Charlotte would be the first to confess that she is not remarkable. Her needs and desires are simple, and by going solo she has found freedom.

Write down what gives you satisfaction in your work and leisure experience. Is there a way to turn your most satisfactory endeavours into a business? Finding your way to a rewarding career is largely a matter of doing what you enjoy. Paraphrasing Buckminister Fuller when he was interviewed, William Sutton stated: "We are too much caught up in setting goals, and when we reach our goals, happiness only lasts for a few moments. It is in the everyday that real living happens. The object of work is to enjoy each day; when you do that, everything else, including money and success, follows."

Dianne Shore is an interior planner who has learned how to buy and sell properties over the years. Dianne is also an experienced renovator and owns a retail shop and restaurant. Dianne began without funds, and now can only estimate the value of her holdings. She has tailored her life to her specifications. She admits that she feels "lucky and blessed," but when you examine the life choices she has made, you see that she's allowed herself to use all her talents. Dianne, like other interior planners, could have chosen to continue working for others, utilizing only the skill the firm she worked for demanded; the design of office interiors. Instead, she went on her own and developed both her talent for design and her talent for real estate.

Ray Kroc did not climb the ladder of corporate success working for someone else. He believed that with the expanding network of highways in North America there was a place for hamburger stands at every highway interchange. He did not have to attend intensive courses at "Hamburger University." He utilized his skills and created McDonald's. As an insurance salesman for many years, he understood the needs of the general public. He was able to offer the public a standard of quality at an inexpensive price.

Edward Land was a researcher in optics, with a certain flair for salesmanship. During World War II, the U.S. Army-Air Force needed a rapid developing film for its reconnaissance flights. Land was able to develop a film that met government standards. When the war ended, he began to make improvements in the film and he created the Polaroid Corporation. The leisure market that followed in the wake of World War II eagerly sought his product, and the company grew to sales in the hundreds of millions. When the government of South Africa began to use Polaroid cameras to make identity cards for purposes of racial identification, the company reacted and boycotted the South African market. The soloist who owns his own business can listen to his conscience too.

When the Reichman brothers created Olympia and York, they utilized the skills they acquired in banking and construction. The creative use of these skills enabled the brothers to finance their buildings at the best possible rates and to construct rapidly.

Creativity is often misunderstood. It is simply bringing into existence that which wasn't there before. The act of cooking dinner is creative. You have an idea what a meal looks like and tastes like; then make the idea a reality.

With a small business, you begin with an idea and start small. Building your business is an adventure along a new path which twists and turns. There are new friends and support, extended learning, new challenges. You begin with a vague notion of the road ahead and work confidently every day until you can map the course.

There is no experience quite like going solo to teach you the ins and outs of the life of the president of any firm. The elements are the same in big business as they are in small business. E.F. Schumacher in his book *Small is Beautiful* points out that the size of many corporations has created a complexity that is totally alien to human living. It takes years to become a competent cog in the industrial wheel. And other areas of endeavour are vulnerable too. The law has become so complicated that it requires eight years of higher education, several years of articling and several more years of working in a law firm in a semi-apprentice position before a lawyer is competent to practise on his own. Both the industrial cog and the lawyer will use only a fraction of their knowledge and skill in their working life. Modern complexity has led to the atrophy of natural and acquired talents. The soloist experiences an awakening of those talents and discovers what it is to be truly involved. Living and working become one.

What you need and desire at forty is not necessarily what you needed and desired at thirty. Only in your own business can you make decisions without the trauma of career changes. Your business is a reflection of yourself, and it changes with you. If it doesn't—if you cease to be enamoured with your work—you can sell your company and go on to something new.

Your knowledge, talent and skills can be rediscovered. They can be marketed, and you can earn a living doing what intrigues you. Choose what you want to do; recognize and utilize your full potential. There is a product or a service that suits just you, and by discovering it, you market your skills.

Chapter 5
Risk Taking

Chairman Mao once said, "Dare to struggle, dare to win." This is a valuable idea whether you are leading a revolution or starting a business. Even capitalists Howard Hughes or Sam Bronfman would not likely take issue with the thought.

Winning can be a struggle, but the rewards are worth the effort. William Sutton was prepared to lose his home and all he owned to make his business work. He was prepared to take maximum risks. His wife supported him emotionally with the words, "If we lose everything, we can build again."

In 1967, Kelly LaBrash was offered a position with the Department of Immigration, running their investigation branch. They offered him over $14,000 a year, which was then a handsome sum. The lure was almost irresistible, but he turned it down because he believed he could do better financially and gain more personal satisfaction from being on his own.

Sandy Simpson of S.L. Simpson Gallery could have taken the traditional route as a researcher in an art gallery, but instead she chose to take a risk and start her own gallery. Her many sales have not yet made her wealthy, but Sandy is twenty-six, and her business is growing.

Can You Take a Risk?

Initiating and managing your own business can be risky, but entrepreneurs adjust to risk taking. Most of them know that if they had not taken their first risk, they would not have found security.

Risk taking is defined by the dictionary as a possible exposure to loss or injury. For the individual with a good attitude toward risk, it is more than that: it is an opportunity. The average soloist (if any soloist can be called average) will maintain that the greater risk is to attempt nothing. Willy Loman in *Death of a Salesman* spent his life selling the products of others. He never had a moment of joy to call his own. It killed him. The play, for the record, is based on a real person. And Willy Loman has many counterparts in reality.

A.P. Giannini could have successfully run his father's green grocery in San Francisco. But for some reason he decided to start a bank. He called it the Bank of Italy and sought to attract Italian depositers in the San Francisco Bay area. The earthquake of 1906 resulted in a fire that wiped out the city, but Giannini, using his deposit base, made low-interest loans to small businessmen so they could rebuild their businesses. Establishment bankers and most investment houses believed that Giannini would go broke as a result of his loan risks. He didn't. The loans helped the city to recover and were quickly repaid. The Bank of Italy grew, and its name was changed to the Bank of America, now one of the largest banks in the world.

The risk taker is bold, willing to gamble on an idea or a belief. The risk taker is willing to challenge what many would call "the impossible."

When you think of mass-marketed language studies, you may think of Berlitz, but Joanna Campion is doing millions of dollars of business each year selling her own language courses. There are few national magazines that do not contain her picture and a description of the services her company offers. The odds were overwhelmingly against the success of her idea. Virtually everyone except Joanna, her husband and her backers believed she would have no chance for success. They were wrong; the market is always open to challengers.

In the mid-1950s two men met in the middle of southern California. Both had heard something about the other, both were working toward a similar end, signing up franchises for their fast-food chains. Ray Kroc of McDonald's and Harlan Saunders of Kentucky Fried Chicken became friends. They were competing for the dollar in the fast-food market, and that dollar went for chicken on one day, hamburgers and fries the next. Each could and did become a success by taking a risk.

Some would say that starting a business in today's economy is an extremely high risk, citing high interest rates, high inflation, increasingly high taxation, and high unemployment. But these same factors make counting on a steady income from a corporation or industry a real risk. Workers appear to have two choices: take no obvious risks and end up among the unemployed, or go solo and create a company that will in turn create jobs. The latter choice in today's economy may be less of a risk than the former.

There is an exhilaration in conscious risk taking. It sharpens your sense of survival. To find out if you are ready to go solo, take the following quiz.

Test Your Risk-Taking Potential

1. Are you willing to enter into debt?

   a. Yes
   b. No

2. If yes, how great a debt?

   a. Below $5,000
   b. $5,000 to 9,999
   c. $10,000 to 19,999
   d. $20,000 to 39,999
   e. More than $40,000

3. Are you comfortable with your present style of living?

   a. All the time
   b. Most of the time
   c. Usually
   d. Seldom
   e. Not at all

4. Whom do you admire most?

   a. General George F. Patton
   b. Pierre Elliott Trudeau
   c. Alan Eagleson
   d. Thomas Edison
   e. None of the above

5. Which casino games do you prefer the most?

    a. Blackjack
    b. Roulette
    c. Craps
    d. Slot machines
    e. None of the above

6. What is your favourite card game?

    a. Bridge
    b. Poker
    c. Gin Rummy
    d. Canasta
    e. None of the above

7. What is your favourite parlor game?

    a. Monopoly
    b. Backgammon
    c. Chess
    d. Checkers
    e. None of the above

8. Do you enjoy electronic video games?

    a. All the time
    b. Most of the time
    c. Usually
    d. Seldom
    e. Not at all

9. Are you comfortable and at ease with strangers?

    a. All the time
    b. Most of the time
    c. Usually
    d. Seldom
    e. Not at all

10. Do you act on the "spur of the moment"?

    a. All the time
    b. Most of the time
    c. Usually
    d. Seldom
    e. Not at all

11. Rank in order of preference:

    a. Career
    b. Family
    c. Self
    d. Community

12. When you find something you like, you stick with it.

    a. True
    b. False

13. You need money to make money.

    a. True
    b. False

14. Success is composed of equal parts of hard work and luck.

    a. True
    b. False

15. Do you consider yourself creative?

    a. All the time
    b. Most of the time
    c. Usually
    d. Seldom
    e. Not at all

16. Do you fantasize about your future?

    a. All the time
    b. Most of the time
    c. Usually
    d. Seldom
    e. Not at all

17. How often do you make mistakes?

    a. All the time
    b. Most of the time
    c. Usually
    d. Seldom
    e. Not at all

18. Do you profit from your mistakes?

    a. All the time
    b. Most of the time
    c. Usually
    d. Seldom
    e. Not at all

19. Did you have a job before the age of 16?

    a. Yes
    b. No

20. Do you create your own opportunities?

    a. All the time
    b. Most of the time
    c. Usually
    d. Seldom
    e. Not at all

21. Are you in control of your future?

    a. All the time
    b. Most of the time
    c. Usually
    d. Seldom
    e. Not at all

22. What do you desire most out of success?

    a. Power
    b. Wealth
    c. Prestige
    d. Early retirement
    e. None of the above

23. Are the "boom years" over?

    a. Yes
    b. No
    c. Undecided

24. Has the world become too complicated?

    a. Yes
    b. No
    c. Undecided

25. Do you envy those people with inherited wealth?

    a. Yes
    b. No
    c. Undecided

26. If you were stranded on a desert island, would you want:

    a. A beautiful woman/handsome man
    b. A *Joy of Cooking* cookbook
    c. An encyclopedia
    d. A Swiss army knife
    e. None of the above

Answer Values: (1) a = 5, b = 0; (2) a = 1, b = 2, c = 3, d = 4, e = 5; (3) a = 2, b = 3, c = 5, d = 3, e = 1; (4) a = 1, b = 0, c = 5, d = 7, e = 4; (5) a = 2, b = 5, c = 3, d = 1, e = 1; (6) a = 2, b = 5, c = 3, d = –1, e = 1; (7) a = 5, b = 3, c = 3, d = 1, e = 1; (8) a = –3, b = 0, c = 2, d = 4, e = 0; (9) a = 7, b = 5, c = 3, d = 2, e = 1; (10) a = 2, b = 3, c = 5, d = 2, e = 1; (11) a = 4, b = 3, c = 5, d = 1; (12) a = 0, b = 2; (13) a = 0, b = 4; (14) a = 0, b = 4; (15) a = 6, b = 4, c = 3, d = 2, e = 1; (16) a = 2, b = 4, c = 5, d = 2, e = 0; (17) a = 0, b = 1, c = 2, d = 5, e = 1; (18) a = 5, b = 3, c = 2, d = 1, e = 0; (19) a = 5, b = 0; (20) a = 5, b = 4, c = 2, d = 1, e = 0; (21) a = 5, b = 3, c = 2, d = 1, e = –2; (22) a = 3, b = 5, c = 2, d = 1, e = 1; (23) a = 0, b = 3, c = 1; (24) a = 0, b = 3, c = 1; (25) a = 0, b = 5, c = 1; (26) a = 2, b = 0, c = 1, d = 5, e = 1.

Analysis of Score:

0 to 25 points: You are cautious almost to a fault. If your debt is average, you fear you will be unable to meet the payments. Your mortgage is up for renewal, and the likelihood is that you will be paying twice as much as before. Rather than explore new methods and approaches of making money, you devote your energies to hoarding whatever you have or will receive. You are willing to accept a reduction in pay because you believe it will save your job.

26 to 50 points: You know that life's a "rat's race," but feel powerless to change it. Your family survived the Great Depression of the 1930s, but just barely. You grew up hearing the stories of how tough it was back then, how so many people in your family were out of work and for how long, and how getting a secure job was the only salvation. You don't truly believe it, especially now. But the childhood conditioning has been intense, and you are hard-pressed to break with your past. You would like to go solo but recognize that your family would be in opposition, and whatever support you might receive would be grudgingly granted. You've worked too long and too hard at your present company to place your future in jeopardy.

51 to 75 points: If you are currently employed, your favourite song is *We've got to get out of this place.* You know that the economy stinks, but you also know that as an employee your position will not substantially improve. Some of your friends and former co-workers have already been going solo for some time. Some have gone bankrupt, but an even greater number have had limited success. You have several "money-making" ideas floating around in your mind, and you have read every business book you could lay your hands on. In theory, you could be a millionaire tomorrow with all you have learned, but you will never truly know until you start going solo. The groundwork has been laid: the methods of financing are reasonably clear in your mind, and you even have a location (one which you have passed driving to work every day). All that is now required is that kick in the rear for you to start going solo. Watch it! The force behind that kick is gradually diminishing.

76 points and above: Your apprenticeship has been completed. Chances are the papers have already been signed and the shingle for your front door is about to be delivered. The only thing that can go wrong is a piano falling on your head, and that only occurs in comic books. You have not felt this eager since you first drove your parents' car, and the world was open for you to explore. If you've made your first solo dollar, you were too busy celebrating or re-investing it to find the time to purchase a frame. Each day is now a celebration as you have taken one more step on the road to independence. You will succeed because you believe in yourself.

Lady Luck

You've probably heard someone say, "Well, Joe was just lucky." Or perhaps you are more familiar with the variation, "Fred had all the contacts, that's why he's a millionaire." Actually, Joe and Fred took a succession of risks, and the risks paid off. Now they are simply "lucky."

Lady Luck has a habit of visiting individuals who can take risks. She has a hard time finding her way to those incapable of risk taking. You have to play to win.

Even within a corporation, luck only visits those who take risks, whether it is a visit to the president to ask for a raise, or an attempt to sell the firm on a new concept, product or product promotion, a new marketing technique or ad campaign.

Andrew Crosbie and Angus MacKay took a risk when they produced their first record. It was a small risk, but luck smiled on them. Angus and Andrew continue to take risks on new recording artists.

Marlys Carruthers, Lynn McLaughlin and Joyce Krusky could have left their recipes securely in their files, but they took a risk and produced their first cookbook. By the act of saying "Yes, we can" and putting hard work behind their risk, all three ladies have substantial bank accounts. Their friends in Calgary thought they were a bit mad at first, but no one thinks so now. Today, they are considered "just lucky."

A risk is a risk, and it is easy to take if you are committed to what you are doing. A half risk is, however, more dangerous than a full risk. A half risk identifies you as one who is holding back, and if you are holding back, you don't have the commitment and the belief in yourself that you will need for success. Joanna Campion spent two years developing her language courses. She made a full commitment and took a complete risk. Joanna is considered "lucky."

Sandy Simpson spent years developing the reputations of the artists she represents. Now after four years of hard work, and a belief in herself and her artistic taste, Lady Luck is smiling on her. She has increased her sales, and the paintings she sells fetch higher prices.

Linda Kuglemass developed her clothing line, Carol Michaud, as the result of a dare. Even though she could not draw or sew, Linda took a full risk. She hired a pattern maker, developed a line of clothing, and then worked incredibly hard, night and day to sell what she had created. When her line sold out and reorders poured in, people said she was "lucky." Linda paid off her bank loans in two months and was then free and clear to take more risks.

Luck comes to those who can take a risk and back their gamble with hard work, belief and planning. The harder you work, the luckier you seem to become.

And who are the unlucky or the luckless? They are those who sell real estate and don't buy a house; those who are filled with ideas for books or television shows but only write one line or a paragraph before they give up. The luckless keep their savings in the bank where they believe it is safe, and the bank uses their money to invest in the high-risk ventures of others. The luckless do not take risks. But a rock can fall on your head even if you are standing still.

The soloists interviewed for this book felt lucky. They felt lucky to be doing work that they found personally satisfying. They felt lucky because they had made money. They felt lucky because they were succeeding.

Luck for Audrey Grant of The Toronto Bridge Club is the pure pleasure of taking care of the extended family she loves, enabling them to have satisfying employment by sharing in the family business. Luck for Nathan Zavier and Lynn Hubacheck is the opportunity to live and make money in interesting ways. For Cathy Deuber of Home Minders, luck is having the ability to fulfill her dream of having a guest house in Bermuda and knowing that the realization of that dream was made possible through her own hard work.

Luck, or what everyone calls luck, can fall to anyone willing to take a risk. Nothing ventured, nothing gained.

The Nay Sayers

Into the life of every risk taker, comes the nay sayer. Nay sayers cannot take risks themselves, and they delight in being around to undermine your enthusiasm. Nay sayers come in many varieties: husbands, wives, mothers, fathers, friends and relations. All have a common attitude, and all are willing to provide hundreds of good, solid, logical reasons why your risk is too risky. They will talk about the economy and high interest rates. They will visit you regularly to see if you are still starving and broke.

Audrey Grant lives with comments such as, "Oh, you're still here! I thought you'd be bankrupt by now." Although she cringes, she has learned to live with thoughtless and negative comments. They are beginning to hurt less as time goes on and her financial status becomes more stable.

As a soloist, you should expect to be considered a little "off the wall," at first. What you're creating is new and untested and, therefore, suspect. Criticism is easy to come by, and being critical enables dependent personalities to feel as if they're accomplishing a mission to save the world by eliminating risk.

When you are getting started and your business is small, nay sayers can be destructive because they create unnecessary doubts. *Avoid nay sayers.* Realize that your company can thrive and that while you will grow rich in freedom, opportunities and money, they will be moving on to others to explain why taking risks is a bad idea. You will find support in the market place and in the act of working for yourself. You are on your way to success. The nay sayers don't matter.

"No" is a lazy word. "No" never made anything happen. Only "Yes, I'll do it" can bring you success.

So develop a tough hide. Close your ears to negative comments, especially those that are based on a lack of understanding of the type of business you are in. Later on, when your risk is paying off, the nay sayers will welcome the chance to work for and with you. They may even want to buy shares in your business.

Chapter 6

Finding the Right Idea

William Sutton of William J. Sutton, Special Risk Insurance, Inc. was fired one day; ten days later he was in business for himself. Sandy Simpson of S.L. Simpson Gallery made effective use of her fine-arts degree. Michael Woods was an accountant in a large firm when one day he hung out his own shingle. These three soloists illustrate how a business can be established when someone simply takes the skills acquired through education and salaried employment and goes it alone.

Are you in a position to go it alone? If you like what you do and you are currently employed as a researcher, an accountant, a bookkeeper, a secretary, a lawyer, a salesperson, a public relations specialist, an ad writer, a technical writer, a butcher, a chemist, a metallurgist, or any one of a hundred other jobs, you *can* become a soloist.

To see if your current profession, vocation or trade lends itself to soloing, ask yourself the following questions:

1. Is there a need for independent workers in my profession, vocation or trade?
2. Could I work out of my home?
3. What are the tax advantages of going it alone in my profession?
4. Do I like my work enough to want to turn it into my own business?
5. Is there room in my field for another independent?
6. Is there some way I can turn my present profession or trade into a unique business?

On this last point, a good plumber with artistic taste, for example, could offer a complete kitchen or bathroom renovation service. Such a service would combine two skills and lend itself to good advertising copy. There are many people who buy sinks or fancy commodes and then can't install them. If, as the installer, you also marketed the equipment, you would be providing a different kind of plumbing service.

The combining of two or more skills is one way of finding the right idea for your own business. One of those skills may grow out of your present salaried employment.

Michael Gowling of Michael Gowling Productions is an example. Michael is in charge of all aspects of his productions: he sells new ideas for effective ways to teach with video, costs out the project, designs his own story boards and does the actual filming. And when Michael hires free lancers for various jobs, he has had experience with what they are doing and so is able to supervise their work.

Dianne Shore is another example of combining skills to create a unique business. Her retail store, The Storeroom, reflects her ability to stock and sell the unusual. Her renovation of the entire corner of Sherbourne and King Street East in Toronto adds to the beauty of the city and illustrates her talent to prospective customers.

But perhaps you will not establish your business or find the right idea by continuing your present profession on your own. Perhaps instead, you will leave all vestiges of your present job behind and pursue a life-long interest. Perhaps you, like photographer Fred Bird, have always cherished the thought of doing something "different" or risky.

> I was always interested in art as a kid, and coming from a farm, I knew that it was better than driving a tractor. I went to the Ontario College of Art in 1960 for a year. For the next twelve years I worked at a number of jobs, mostly in advertising and the graphic arts. I didn't even hold a camera in my hand until I was in my mid-twenties.
>
> By the late 1960s, I was working as a sales representative for a large art studio. They had a damn good photographer at the studio. My job was to do the selling and, after the sale was made, do the design work and create the sets. When the sets were completed, the photographer would take the pictures. I always believed he was having more fun at his job than I was at mine.
>
> One day he didn't show up for an assignment, and the account executive asked me to take the shots. I didn't know what the hell I was doing, but I walked through it. After that it

> was easy. I knew that I wanted to be a photographer, so all I had to do was master all that technical garbage. Once you learn how all the machines operate, the rest is easy.

Many soloists find their inspiration in their hobbies. One day they realize that the hobby they have devoted themselves to for years is what they really enjoy, and they say, "Hey, I think I can make a living out of this."

Do you dream of spending more time on your hobby? A person who desires nothing more than to write full-time can take advantage of many opportunities even though the competition is great. The person who likes to read may make an ideal free-lance researcher and can earn a good hourly wage.

Dennis Adair and Janet Rosenstock of Freelance Writing Associates, Inc. began their writing business by specializing in educational materials. Corporations interested in providing educational materials for schools hired them to write, and they soon produced pamphlets and study materials for Imperial Oil, General Foods, Colgate, Kraft, and thirty-five other large corporations. Before they teamed up, they both had taught and worked at a variety of jobs. But the day they teamed up they began as full-time writers and took maximum risks.

Art Smolensky is one of the most educated soloists we interviewed. He holds a Ph.D. from the University of British Columbia in chemistry, but he has always been interested in photography. Now he is the owner of a chain of photography stores on the lower mainland of British Columbia.

Audrey Grant owns a bridge club in Toronto. She has always loved the game of bridge and enjoys her job of bringing diverse people together for an evening of fun and relaxation.

One young man was a tireless collector of tacky posters, postcards, furniture, costumes and bar-room decorations, all *circa* 1900. He turned his collection into a thriving store. Doesn't everyone want to own a mirror that advertises beer and is decorated with purple feathers?

Next comes pure inspiration, and Gary Dahl's Pet Rock certainly makes a fine example. To it can be added a long list of money-makers that includes the Hula Hoop, the Frisbee, wacky stationary, personalized pens and pencils, obscene ashtrays and beer openers, toilet paper with profound and not-so-profound messages, plastic creatures from outer space and items too absurd to mention. To sell an idea that is based on pure inspiration you may have to have a bit of P.T. Barnum in you, but most entrepreneurs have more than a little of Barnum's personality and outlook.

The above examples are unusual, but there are quite ordinary needs to be filled. Cathy Deuber's Home Minders was a unique idea for a personal service at the time she began her business. Most people sent their animals to kennels or asked neighbours to look after them. Today Cathy is making money pet-sitting. The animals are happier, and the customers get more for their money than they would from a kennel.

Read to find ideas for your own business. You'll be surprised at the number of books filled with money-making ideas. And in addition to ideas, you'll find all the how-to information you need to get started. For example, you might start with Don Kracke's book *How to Turn Your Idea Into a Million Dollars*. This valuable volume covers patenting ideas and selling your wares yourself, or to a distribution company for a royalty.

If this doesn't sound like important information, think a moment about the bank employee who created the system for computerized chequing accounts—all those little numbers on the bottom of your cheques. He was an employee at the time he developed his system, and once his bank began using it, the other banks did as well. Because he was employed at the time, he did not patent his program. Later, he went to court and sued for royalties. It was estimated that if he was granted a royalty of one cent per cheque book, the banks would owe him seven billion dollars. An out-of-court settlement was reached for several million. This happened a number of years ago, but it illustrates the importance of patenting unique ideas whether they be inventions or computer programs.

Read *Forbes* magazine as well as *Money* and other financial publications. The more you read about the economy the greater will be your understanding of how to make and spend money. Regardless of whether you pursue your own business as the result of evolution, inspiration or the fulfillment of a dream, you need to understand finance. The soloists interviewed recognized the necessity to understand finance. What they did not understand initially became apparent as they progressed. As Michael Gowling pointed out: "The 1980s is the decade of information. In the past it was the "haves" and the "have-nots." In the 1980s, it's the "knows" and "know-nots." Know and you stand a good chance of success. Know-not and you will be running a risk that is easily avoidable.

Openness to experience can lead you to an idea for a business venture. *Successful business is simply finding a need and filling it.*

As people shy away from big new purchases, the person with a talent for repairing and reconditioning furniture, appliances and other items is in demand. If you take your $100 vacuum cleaner back to the department store for repairs, it may cost you $50. If you trade it to a reconditioner, you get a completely reconditioned vacuum cleaner for $25. Large appliances often come with repair contracts, but there is a considerable sum to be made in the reconditioning of small appliances.

Henry Ford realized people needed an inexpensive car in order to get around. He took a car apart, put it back together and created mass automobile production. Ray Kroc believed that with reasonable cars, excellent highways and the need to eat on the go, there should be inexpensive restaurants offering a standardized menu. McDonald's was created.

Webster's defines "free lance" as "a knight or roving soldier available for hire by a state or commander; one who pursues a profession under no long-term contractual commitments to any one employer." It was this definition that prompted Dennis Adair and Janet Rosenstock to name their corporation Freelance Writing Associates, Inc. They always enjoyed writing, and since they began in the mid-1970s, they have written pamphlets on soap, cat food, soft drinks, chewing gum, toothpaste, foreign aid, and many other subjects as well as study sheets on educational films. The variety of knowledge and experience they garnered in preparing such pamphlets have assisted them in their writing of full-length fiction and non-fiction.

Free lancers performing tasks needed by industry are able to make considerable sums of money. Many corporations can no longer afford to have hundreds of employees on staff because each salary multiplies itself with the cost of benefits and pensions. If you can write a brochure, there are hundreds of companies willing to give you an assignment and pay you well.

In addition to being hired by corporations for a variety of

tasks, there is reciprocity between free lancers. Rather than assume the overheads, both financial and administrative, of having a large staff, many soloists simply farm their work out to free lancers. Whenever Michael Gowling needs typing done, he calls on a typing service with a word processor so that he can keep track of his letters. When he needs a letter sent, Michael simply calls the typing service, they pull the appropriate disk and make the changes he desires, and the letter is completed. Michael does not have to worry about employees and their accompanying problems, and he is usually assured of a job well done. The superior quality of work and the savings in overhead are a boon; higher profits are the result.

People in business for themselves have a strong vested interest in doing the job right and doing the job on time. Their productivity is high because their own reputations are on the line. Perhaps you can find an idea for your business by finding out the needs of other small-business people.

Look to the changes in the economy when you search for an idea for a business of your own. Perhaps you want to own a company that provides secretarial services or translation service. Quality work and prompt service can virtually guarantee you an income if you select the right area.

The economy may be in dire straits, but there is still work to be done and money to be earned. The economic structure may require a rethinking of methods of earning a living. Going solo can be a flexible alternative for those displaced by technology or declared redundant by debt-ridden companies.

You may begin to build a business on one idea, and as you progress, new ideas and opportunities may occur to you. Cathy Deuber was going to operate a franchise for Merle Norman Cosmetics. She travelled to California to study their methods. When Cathy returned to Canada, she went to work for a company called Home Minders. She needed some extra cash and the time to consider the possibilities with Merle Norman. Cathy wound up buying Home Minders instead. Under her guidance, the company has reached a point where franchises are being offered and sold throughout Ontario.

To get off the treadmill of working for others, you must begin the search for a money-making venture that will bring you satisfaction. You may even pick up odd jobs here and there while you are searching. To find the right idea, you must be open to all opportunities, and you must allow your mind full creative range. One day you may find yourself sitting with a pad of paper scribbling down an idea for an all-weather jacket just perfect for the cold winters and wet springs in Canada. The next day you might be working out the details of a new toy or pastime. In the meantime, you may be envying the money made by a free-lance delivery service and decide that you too could make money in that area.

How do soloists know when the idea is right? According to some entrepreneurs such as Eunice Webster, "You just know." Other soloists research their ideas, do test marketing, and pilot programs.

A soloist must exert self-discipline in the matter of choosing an idea to pursue. Novelists are instructed to be careful about selecting a theme for a novel because the discipline of writing over a long period of time requires that a novelist "live with the theme and the characters on a day-to-day basis." This same principle holds true for the soloist. A soloist may be able to shift gears more quickly than a large corporation, but he or she cannot simply jump ship after a bad day, continually changing direction and never allowing any one concept to grow.

If you decide to create and market stationery, you have to live with all phases of your idea. You start with paper design, you contact box manufacturers, create a prototype, spend weeks making sales calls to get orders, manufacture the stationery, spend time or money filling and delivering the boxes, invoicing and following up on payments and on and on till your profit on each box sold represents a substantial gain. What is required is enthusiasm for every step in the process, and if the enthusiasm isn't there, success will not be there either. You can't just make a few boxes for friends and family and wonder why your idea didn't pay off.

As a soloist, you must present your product or service with real vitality, have an enthusiasm for hard work and have total commitment to the product or service. You must be able to live with the idea and recognize the fact that you will not really know whether it can support you until you've tried it. You must also accept that it may take you hundreds of phone calls and personal meetings before you receive the acceptance you're seeking. Just remember that Margaret Mitchell, the author of *Gone With the Wind*, was rejected by thirty-eight publishers. The thirty-ninth bought the book.

Look toward your family to help when evaluating an idea for a solo occupation. When Don Kracke and his wife thought up the idea for plastic sticky flowers in the mid-sixties, the whole family was called on for advice. Everyone worked to make Rickie, Tickie, Stickies a success. Laurie, Gail and Brad Greenwood of Greenwood's Books in Edmonton work together as a family. The three have ordinary sibling problems, but when it comes to business the fact that Gail is the oldest makes no difference. Gail's opinion is valued equally with Laurie's and Brad's. All three work hard, with one goal in mind: the success of the business. They also work hard at understanding and respecting each of the other's individual skills. They all make a contribution to the growth of their business.

A group of individuals who enjoy advertising can combine talents as individual small businesses working together for the mutual profit of all. A creative director who's skilled at developing selling campaigns can combine his talents with those supplied by free lancers in sales and secretarial. A money-making advertising firm can be the result.

Knowledge can be gained academically or by practical application. We have long accepted the fact that electricians and plumbers apprentice for their accreditation. But apprenticeship can be well applied in other professions as well.

Many ideas for a small business are self-evident. There is a certain validity and guarantee of success going with the idea that evolves out of life-experience and education. Many recommend going with your experience and adapting that experience to a solo occupation. But there are many individuals who want to try something completely new, and trying something new can be exhilarating. Nancy Thomson decided to go with her new found interest—money and finance—and succeeded in developing an eight-week course for women through extensive study and a utilization of her background as an organizer and teacher.

To find the right idea for your own company, do not ask: "What can I do to make a million?" Instead ask, "What do I really want to do? How can I do it? How can I spend my days involved in satisfying labour?"

The money follows the dream. Many people think, "If I do this task that I hate doing, I'll have millions of dollars to do what I want." You won't. If you do what you really want, then you give of yourself sincerely and your commitment to success is far greater than if you were merely marking time. Ask yourself the following questions about your idea:

- Does the idea thrill and excite me?
- Will my excitement carry me through good times and bad times?
- Will I feel motivated every morning?
- Do I believe in myself enough to carry through with my plans?

If you have answered "yes" to the above questions, you probably have an idea that will work for you. You must have a belief in your idea and its worthiness. No one else can provide this. Now move, step by step:

1. Analyze and evaluate your lifetime of experience.
2. Keep yourself open at all times. You never know where a workable idea may come from.
3. Put your ideas down on paper and test them on friends.
4. Check the competition. Is your service or product unique?
5. Don't be afraid to explain or defend your idea to third parties. They may shoot it down, but remember the last time they presented an idea to you?
6. Make minimum and maximum lists of what you need to get started.
7. Avoid discouragement at all costs! Always think and believe that success can always happen.
8. Trust your instincts.

Remember, to know success you don't have to invent something as outlandish as the Pet Rock, as huge as McDonald's or as useful as the Ford. You have to create or offer a service that is useful. Then you have to design a unique way to make people realize why it is useful.

Chapter 7

Getting Started

On January 9, 1870, the Standard Oil Company did not exist. It was created the next day. John D. Rockefeller had an idea on which he was willing to take a risk. With careful planning what would soon become the largest company in the world was initiated.

John Davison Rockefeller was a commission merchant in Cleveland, Ohio, in the early 1860s. The first oil wells were drilled in nearby northwestern Pennsylvania, and Rockefeller had the foresight to see their potential. He built his first refinery in 1863 and by 1865 his refinery was the largest in the area. His endeavour was incorporated as the Standard Oil Company of Ohio in 1870.

Rockefeller brought efficient methods to the oil business, and much of his success was based on his ability to negotiate favourable freight rates. The profit was, after all, not in taking oil out of the ground or even in refining it. The profit was made when the oil was sold, and Rockefeller knew that how much he paid to get the oil to market directly affected his profits. In short, he took the total picture into consideration.

Inherent in Rockefeller's success story are certain principles:

- Recognition of the value of a product or service.
- Readying the product or service for immediate use.
- Getting the product or service to the customer.
- Creating new markets for the product or service.
- Recognizing the *future* value of the product or service.

Less than two hundred years ago, most products were manufactured with hand tools and required much hand labour. Then industrialization enabled mass production. At the same time, it should be noted, the population of the world increased rapidly, thus providing ever-expanding markets for mass-produced consumer goods. The industrial revolution is romantically known as the "age of the entrepreneur," because the most important factor in the history of industrialization was the *idea* and the people who made ideas reality. Rockefeller had an idea, and he had an opportunity. To these two factors, he added skill.

Another such industrial giant was a Canadian named John J. McLaughlin. In 1890, McLaughlin graduated from university in chemistry. He opened a small plant in Toronto to manufacture soda water (carbonated water), and he sold his product in syphons to drugstore soda fountains, the most important gathering place of young people. This, he quickly realized, was a small market compared to the one he could create if a carbonated drink could be made "portable." At the same time, McLaughlin began to experiment with flavouring extracts.

But it was marketing that troubled McLaughlin most. Canada is a large country, and outside the urban areas there were no drugstores. If people could not get to his market, he would have to find a way to take his product to them. He developed a technique for putting his soda water in bottles, and he began mass production. One of his first products was "McLaughlin Belfast Style Ginger Ale." Ginger was a popular flavour at the turn of the century, just as it is today.

McLaughlin was not entirely satisfied with his products, and on a vacation in France, he sampled French wines and champagnes. He liked the dryness of champagnes as well as their sparkling appearance. Not only did the idea for a new product come to mind, but he developed virtually an entire advertising campaign. A drink that was cold, sparkling and not too sweet. A drink for long, hot summers from "the great north country." Canada Dry was conceived in McLaughlin's mind, and shortly, "Canada Dry Ginger Ale, The Champagne of Ginger Ales," was created.

J.J. McLaughlin's research was not unique. He did not create the soft drink as such. His work was based on the work of chemists who came before him, men such as Joseph Priestly, Benjamin Sillinan and Joseph Hawkins. But J.J. McLaughlin built on their research and ideas. He applied mass production methods. He was concerned with expanding his market, and he found in Canada's image an ideal advertising gimmick. In the beginning was the idea, next an understanding of the current market, then an idea for expanding that market, and finally the ideal selling technique.

And while J.J. McLaughlin was revolutionizing the soft drink industry in Canada and launching a successful business in the United States, his brother was setting up the forerunner of General Motors of Canada. Were these men unusual? Did they have some special gene? Were they simply born at the "right time"? Were they just lucky?

None of the above. All entrepreneurs are a little unusual, but none of them have special genes. They make the time right, and people always say they're lucky. Today's opportunities are no less than yesterday's, and the principles of "getting started" remain the same.

Growing up in the aftermath of World War II, we were taught to believe that the mighty corporations and industrial giants were created by super-heroes, endowed with qualities beyond those of mortal men. *Not true*! The Rockefellers, the McLaughlins and the Bronfmans were and are as mortal as the rest of us.

Modern historical analysts place those Captains of Industry in a period we are told no longer exists. Rockefeller's biographer, Allan Nevins, called it "the age of expansion" and claimed the age was over, believing that high taxes, government regulations and stiffer competition both in home and in foreign markets have made it almost impossible to equal their success.

The young founder of "Apple Computers" would doubtlessly disagree. A multimillionaire in his twenties, he had an idea, and he went after almost exactly the same market as J.J. McLaughlin. People don't take as many computers home as they take home soft drinks, but the cost of computers makes one per family a nice goal to work toward. This is large-scale soloing of course, but one never knows when small-scale soloing will become large. The principles are the same.

Nancy Thomson carefully calculated gradual plans for the growth and expansion of her business. When hundreds of women signed up for her courses, she was pleasantly taken aback. The bookstore of Brad, Gail and Laurie Greenwood may never be a Coles or a Classics, but it is their own. It reflects their vision of what a bookstore can be and also reflects their vision of personal service. Walter Schroeder is proud of the fact that his company is responsible for evaluating giant corporations. He enjoys being a "referee of the money market."

Few, if any, of the soloists interviewed for this book will ever amass the wealth and power of the Rockefellers, the McLaughlins or the Bronfmans. But they will know success. They will apply the principles applied by the supremely successful, and they will have a level of freedom that is not enjoyed by the salaried employee.

Initiating your business venture requires a painstaking period of planning. And your early decisions are of vital importance because how you begin will effect you for years to come. You must think it out step by step.

First, you have your idea or inspiration. The next steps in the establishment of your business are technical. You must decide on the *nature of your company*. Is it to be a sole proprietorship, a partnership or a corporation? How much training, if any, do you need before you open your doors? Do you require a staff? What do you need in terms of seed money? What kind of terms can you obtain from suppliers (if necessary)? Will you pay C.O.D., or can you pay for needed materials in thirty or sixty days? What kind of image will your business project? How will you get your product or service to the consumer? What do you need for the tax department? What kind of certification do you need from the government (federal, provincial or local)? What kind of certification might you need from business associations? How will your customers verify your reliability?

The latter are points you may not have thought of, and while the need for various certifications do not exist in all areas of endeavour, they do exist in many. For example, the federal government gives grants under the C.H.I.P. program to help Canadians upgrade the insulation in their homes in order to save fuel, and because these grants are available, a number of small insulation businesses have sprung up. A *reliable* insulation company will be a member of the Better Business Bureau, will be bonded (because the installers of the insulation have access to your home), will have a local license from the municipal government in most Canadian jurisdictions, will be fully insured against damage they might do to your home, and will be a member of Canadian General Standards Board. (The latter organization insures all workmanship and materials for a period of ten years.)

This is just one example of necessary certifications. Such certifications are necessary for many involved in home repairs, renovations, plumbing, electrical work, etc. Consider the cost of certifications because if they are necessary in your business, you cannot successfully market your product without them.

Finding and Using a Lawyer

It is absolutely vital to retain the services of a lawyer in the initial stages of setting up your business. For most people, experience with the law is limited to paying parking tickets, and experience with lawyers is limited to the making of wills, obtaining mortgages, purchasing a home and possibly getting a divorce.

Setting up a business properly is as important as any of the above. When you are going solo, you are suddenly confronted by a plethora of rules and regulations. The various levels of government have enacted legislation covering aspects of all kinds of businesses. Those involved in food preparation (caterers, restaurants, fresh food shops, etc.) all have regulations to follow which are laid down by local and provincial health departments. In some jurisdictions this includes such factors as medical clearances. Food handlers in some places must be proven not to be typhoid carriers, for example. All businesses have rules, and most have some regulatory authorities.

It may be that the mass of legalities will have little direct effect on your business. But you must be certain. In preparing for day one, you may be signing leases, entering into contractual agreements with suppliers and committing yourself on a variety of levels. Better safe than sorry.

You must understand what you are signing. You must know if your rights are fully protected by contracts, and you must know if your *form* of business organization is suited to the needs of your business.

For all these reasons, you need a lawyer to advise you. One of your friends has probably needed a lawyer in the recent past, and if your friend was satisfied with the service, this may be an ideal recommendation. *However*, you must be aware that while law is a speciality in itself, lawyers themselves specialize in much the same way doctors do. You would not consult a podiatrist for possible brain surgery, nor a urologist for a heart condition. By the same token, you would not hire a criminal lawyer for contracts, nor a real estate lawyer for tax form expertise. A good contract lawyer will probably fill your bill, but try to find one who has some knowledge of your type of business. If you are in a rarified business, look harder. There are corporate lawyers who specialize in corporate contracts and liabilities; there are entertainment lawyers who specialize in film, book and actors' contracts; there are real estate lawyers; lawyers who know health regulations; and many other specialists.

If you do not have access to a contracts lawyer or you require a lawyer with a speciality, call or write your provincial law society. They can provide you with a list, and they will advise you on fee schedules.

These are the eight factors that govern legal fees:

1. The amount of time expended by the solicitor.
2. The legal complexity of the work to be done.
3. The degree of responsibility assumed by the solicitor.
4. The monetary value of matters in dispute (this applies to suits).
5. The importance of the case to the client.
6. The degree of competence shown by the solicitor.
7. Results.
8. The client's ability to pay. (A recent judgement has cast this factor in doubt.)

In Ontario and in other jurisdictions as well, the client who feels he or she has been overcharged may file a complaint with the Taxing Master and have the complaint "taxed"—that is, reviewed—by the Taxing Master. (The authority that reviews overcharging by lawyers can be contacted through provincial law societies.) You do not require a lawyer for this procedure, and it is important that you know you have recourse in the event you feel you have been overcharged.

As an example of a lawyer's fees and how they should be delineated for the client, the following is a *Statement of Account* for a recent incorporation:

For Professional Services Rendered:
For receipt of instructions to act on your behalf;

For initial interview;
For discussion with respect to corporate name;
For advising with respect to share structure and capitalization;
For drafting application for Articles of Incorporation;
For reviewing Articles;
For drafting organizational resolutions;
For drafting by-laws;
For reviewing banking resolution documents;
For attending upon you for execution of all by-laws, resolutions and banking documents;
For correspondence with your accountant with respect to share structure;
For preparing registers in minute book;
For obtaining minute book, seal, by-laws and share certificates;
For completing share certificates;
For preparing shareholders agreement between principals;
For reporting to you and all other necessary and incidental advices;

Our Fee For All of the Above	$500.00
Disbursements:	
Paid Corporation's Fee	$200.00
Paid re: minute book	30.00
Paid for desk seal	25.00
Paid for by-laws	4.00
Paid re: name search	30.00
Paid re: share certificates	6.00
Paid re: mileage (42 km. @ .20¢)	8.40
	303.40
Total Fee and Disbursements	$803.40

If the thought of doing all this gives you a headache, let us assure you it took less than three hours of the client's time. It all sounds infinitely more complicated than it is for the client. This account is included only to illustrate what a legal bill may look like, and how it should be broken down. Remember, lawyers' fees are regulated by the law society and are public knowledge.

Forms of Organization

In the next few pages we will briefly discuss the various forms of business ventures you might enter into. This section is not written by a lawyer, and the information herein is gleaned from experience and research. Definitions, rules and regulations are often changed, and this is a general discussion which involves broad general concepts. None of the information below is the word of the law. Check with your lawyer for legal information.

Sole Proprietorship: As a sole proprietor doing business under your own name, you must register your company with a government regulatory agency or ministry. The cost of registering a sole proprietorship is minimal and varies from one jurisdiction to another. Make certain you have obtained all licenses that may be necessary and that you have complied with all requirements of federal, provincial and local authorities.

There are favourable tax advantages for the sole proprietor, and you can obtain various bulletins that deal with them from Revenue Canada. Even if you acquire an accountant (see Chapter Seven), you will want to examine these advantages for yourself so you will know what specific questions to ask.

The disadvantages of sole proprietorship are more significant for some business ventures than others. As a sole proprietor you carry unlimited liability. If you are sued for any reason, it is you, personally, who is sued, not a company, because all contracts are entered into under your name. Should a judgement go against you, you are fully liable for costs (sometimes these costs include the other lawyer's fee and court costs as well as the amount involved in the suit).

If you go to a bank for financing as a sole proprietor, you may only be able to secure a personal loan. The bank doesn't want to lose its money if you are sued. It is often easier to receive outside financing if you are incorporated.

Also important when considering sole proprietorship is the nature of the business and the size of the business.

You may find it advantageous to begin with a sole proprietorship and incorporate in one or two years as your business grows and stabilizes.

Partnerships: A partnership bears some resemblance to sole proprietorship in that the partners have unlimited liability. Also, the costs of registering a partnership are minimal; you and your partner register together. But a partnership is a complex organizational form of business.

The tax laws are complicated though favourable: partners must file jointly, and income as well as assets, depreciation, expenses, capital loss and capital gain are shared equally.

In so far as government regulations are concerned, a partnership is as regulated as any other form of organization. Regulations depend largely on the type of business rather than the organizational form it takes (with the exception of the tax regulations which vary with the different types of organizational forms). For example, two partners opening a food service are subject to the same health laws as a corporation or a sole proprietor. The main legal difference between a partnership or a sole proprietorship and a corporation is in the matter of liability, and this is a vital difference.

When you establish a partnership, there are also human elements to consider. These include division of authority and responsibility, as well as the simple question, "Will we continue to get along well, operating within a business structure?"

Legally, there are various types of partnerships to be considered. *General partners* have full liability with all their possessions for all the firm's obligations. Usually a general partnership is composed of two *active partners*, but there may be silent, dormant or sleeping partners. These are all legal terms, and it's wise to know that silent, dormant or sleeping partners all share the firm's liability. An ostensible partner is one who lends his name to a firm; he too has full liability under the law.

Some jurisdictions permit limited (or special) partners. A person may invest money in an unincorporated firm and limit his liability to no more than the amount of his investment. There are special requirements for the limited or special partner, and unless all of them are met, the limited or special partner can become completely liable.

Legal regulations apply to the dissolution of partnerships, to one partner leaving, to liability on joint contracts, to new partners entering an existing partnership and to many other facets of this form of organization. Special care must be taken in the matter of distribution of partnership assets, in liabilities (bills incurred jointly) and in the matter of the death or retirement of the partners.

Again, a partnership can be a useful initial organizational structure for the small business. But if the business grows and becomes higly profitable or if it is a business likely to incur large debts or legal actions, incorporation should be considered carefully.

Incorporation: When a business incorporates, it places either "Ltd." or "Inc." after its name. Inc. is the American legal word that indicates *limited liability*; Ltd. (limited) is the British term. Both Inc.'s and Ltd.'s exist in Canada, and legally there is no difference between them. They both have limited liability, which essentially means that those who are incorporated are limited in liability to the amount they have invested in the firm. For example, if $5,000 were invested, the liability would be $5,000.

A company can incorporate either federally, under the Dominions Companies Act, or provincially, under the Provincial Corporations Act. In law, a corporation is almost equal to an individual. It has a name, an office, its own capital, and it sues and gets sued in its own name.

To incorporate properly, you must use a lawyer. It can be done on one's own, but this is an extraordinary risk, since there are many items to be considered and the incorporation forms are hideously complicated.

The incorporated company possesses the legal machinery to obtain financing and that financing is limited only by the amount of public confidence placed in the company. Financing can be obtained from many people by issuing shares. The value of shares cannot, however, exceed the *authorized* capital specified in the charter, but this can be set at virtually any amount. Common shares and bonds can be issued by a corporation. The selling of shares is regulated, and it is wise to understand all you can about your own incorporation. When you incorporate, you are assigned a specific number of shares in the company. If you sell more shares than you, yourself, own, you can lose control. Shareholders have rights and these rights are laid out specifically in the firm's charter and in the law.

Incorporation offers many advantages. For example, it is easier to obtain bank loans because the corporation has limited liability. The tax laws also favour the corporation. Many soloists interviewed did not take salaries from their corporations. Their legitimate day-to-day expenses were covered by the corporation.

The corporation is closely regulated, and it is the most costly form of business organization to initiate (though often the tax advantages pay for this initiation in one year). By regulation a corporation *must* have an accountant and a lawyer. Reports must be sent to the government on a yearly basis. Your corporate charter must state the nature and intention of your business, and while there is no problem doing what you stated, you may find it difficult to branch out. This is where your lawyer comes in. When you obtain your charter, you can include a number of potential areas. A writer, for example, might choose to have a charter that enables his company to publish, to edit, to consult, to research, to teach other writers, to be involved in film and television and to agent. The broader the base, the better.

The choice of organizational structure depends on the nature of the business. Fred Bird and Michael Woods began their businesses one way and then incorporated.

Fred Bird: I started out in a partnership with another man. He had the business head, and I was the creative one with the sales contacts. Toward the end of our partnership we fought all the time. We dissolved the partnership while calling each other a "bastard." With the help of my lawyer, I bought the other guy out. My lawyer took care of the incorporation, and within a few days of dissolution, Fred Bird and Associates Limited was created.

Michael Woods: Entering business with a partner relieves much of the fear and anxiety when you are starting out. In my case, the business already existed, and there was a client base.

From the moment I walked in the door on day one, there was work to be done. Financial statements had to be prepared, and clients were already scheduled for appointments through-

> out the week. My major fear, at the start, was not cash or lack of business, but my own ability to get the job done. The fear lasted as long as it took me to state it. I had no choice but to get down to work.

It is still possible to get started and to earn a good living working for yourself. The age of the industrial giants is not over; nor is the age of expansion or the age of the entrepreneur. Idea, need, the creation of need and hard work can get you started.

Checklist on Getting Started

1. Obtain a lawyer. You never know when you might need one, so you might as well utilize a lawyer's services from the beginning. At the very least, you will receive some concrete advice on what form of business organization serves your needs. If you choose to incorporate, you will require a lawyer in any case.
2. Register your firm at the appropriate ministry and obtain all other certificates, accreditations, licenses or other documents needed for your specific business.
3. Make a detailed list of everything you have to do before day one. Don't be shy about including the mundane. Your list should include everything from financing to the purchase of a pencil sharpener. You'll find that if you begin with basic checklists, you'll get into the habit. There's too much to remember to trust your memory.
4. Don't be afraid to ask about what you do not know. You are still sailing uncharted waters; so borrow a compass.
5. Keep studying. Libraries and bookstores are filled with books and pamphlets that will tell you everything you need to know.

Where to Register Your Company

Federal

Department of Consumer and Corporate Affairs,
Place du Portage,
Hull, P.Q. K1A 0C9
(819) 997-2938

Alberta

Department of Consumer and Corporate Affairs,
Room 224,
Legislative Building,
Edmonton, Alberta T5K 2B6
(403) 427-9883

British Columbia

Ministry of Consumer and Corporate Affairs,
940 Blanshard Street,
Victoria, B.C. V8W 3E6
(604) 387-1251

Manitoba

Department of Consumer and Corporate Affairs and Environment,
Legislative Building,
Winnipeg, Man. R3C 0V8
(204) 944-3746

New Brunswick

Department of Justice,
Room 216,
Centennial Building,
Fredericton, N.B. E3B 5H1
(506) 453-2589

Newfoundland

Department of Justice,
Confederation Building,
St. John's, Nfld. A1C 5T7
(709) 737-2890

Nova Scotia

Department of the Attorney General,
Box 7,
Halifax, N.S. B3J 2L6
(902) 424-4223

Ontario

Ministry of Consumer and Corporate Affairs,
555 Yonge Street,
Toronto, Ontario M7A 2H6
(416) 963-1111

Prince Edward Island

Department of Justice and Attorney General,
Box 2000,
Charlottetown, P.E.I. C1A 7N8
(902) 892-5411

Quebec

Department of Industry, Trade & Tourism
1 Place Ville-Marie, 23rd Floor
Montreal, P.Q. H3B 3M6
(418) 643-5084
or
710, Place d'Youville,
Quebec, P.Q. G1R 4Y4
(418) 643-5084

Saskatchewan

Department of Consumer and Commercial Affairs,
1871 Smith Street,
Regina, Sask. S4P 3V7
(306) 565-5577

Chapter 8
Financing Your Company

The amount of capital required to initiate your own business can range from zero upward to hundreds of thousands of dollars depending on the type of business you create. A business devoted to a personal service or one that grows out of a purely creative endeavour (writing, painting, music) may cost very little to get started. A business that requires the purchase or production of merchandise can cost a good deal more.

Financial savvy can be learned on the job, but you should be prepared to consider a number of alternatives in the primary stages of financing, and you should understand the implications of some of the more common alternatives.

Preparation

There are no hard and fast rules in the matter of financial preparation for launching your own business. Again, the amount of seed money you require depends on the nature of the business and the length of time you estimate it will take to bring in income. You may need sufficient funding to care for yourself and your family for six months or a year. Or, you may need money to actually begin your business. If, on the other hand, your business will begin paying you almost immediately, you may need very little. Michael Woods, the solo accountant, falls into the latter category. He had assignments when he hung out his shingle and was probably no more than thirty days from collecting his first fees. Doug Dunbar of College Copy Shop, on the other hand, needed to purchase and lease the equipment necessary to make his business a success. This required an immediate outlay of cash; thus he had to raise money to open his doors for business.

The first preparation for financing is to make three lists:

Personal Assets: include the equity you have in your home (if you own one), all property, your car or cars (if you are still paying for them, include only your equity), your furniture, jewellery, personal savings, stocks or bonds—in short, your total net worth.

Personal Liabilities: include *all* personal bills and your total living expenses for one month. Do not forget insurance payments (write down the month in which these come due), car payments and mortgage payments if any.

Future Personal Liabilities: include your monthly expenses for however long you estimate it will be before you have an income. Then add three months. Be sure to include such things as university tuition if you have a teenager who will begin university during your launching period. Try to see into the future and make your list as comprehensive as possible, giving yourself leeway for emergencies.

Now you should make three similar lists for your proposed business. To these lists you might add a fourth column: *Potential Income*. This list would include any assignments or contracts you consider to be "in the bag" but not yet under actual contract. Your assets will be whatever money you intend to invest or borrow (this amount should not appear on your personal assets list). Your liabilities will include the costs of legal fees, registration, certification if necessary, professional dues if necessary, licenses if necessary, interest on bank loans if applicable and whatever money you require to get started in terms of equipment, material or salaries for personnel.

You should start small with an eye to expansion. The single biggest danger to the new soloist is *overextension* of resources. Overextension is the cause of most bankruptcies, large and small. While overextension for a large company may be 4.3 billion, for the soloist $20,000 can be just as dangerous. This word of caution does not mean you should be unwilling to take risks, but there is a difference between taking a risk and being foolhardy.

The next list to devise is what might be called a personal asset list, and it does not involve money. It is a list of what you personally bring to your business. For example, William J. Sutton spoke of the support he had from people in the insurance business, support he earned while working for others. They were willing to help him, so he brought "good will" with him to his own business. Sharon James, a caterer, brought her reputation. Reputation *is* an asset.

These lists will help you and your accountant (don't forget his fees) to prepare a proposal for financing if such a proposal is necessary. Banks look more kindly on those who estimate their expenses accurately and allow a realistic amount for unexpected contingencies.

If you incorporate, there is a factor you should be aware of when you finance your company. *Limited liability* does not mean no liability. You are liable *up to the amount you invest in your corporation.* If you invest $5,000, you are liable for $5,000. If you invest $50,000, you are liable for $50,000. If you claim that you have brought $20,000 worth of good will to your corporation for tax purposes, that $20,000 becomes a part of your investment and a part of your liability. If you do not take a salary, the amount you reinvest in the corporation on paper becomes a part of your investment and a part of your liability. Incorporation is the safest form of business organization, but it is wise to remember that what the law gives with one hand, it takes away with the other.

A soloist who initiates a low overhead business may need no more than enough to pay for registration and food for, say, a six-month period (plus utility bills and a little spending money). It may be worthwhile to follow the Mormons, who traditionally have a policy of always keeping a six-month supply of food on hand for each member of their family. They do this in order to protect themselves from acts of "man and God." If a Mormon loses his job, he knows he at least has six months of meals for himself and his family, during which he can get back on his feet. A Mormon's savings account usually provides for the same contingency. The mortgage, car payments, fuel, repairs and even the odd book can be purchased. Such planning ahead is important because the soloist starting out should not have to worry constantly about day-to-day survival.

Sources of Financial Help

Doug Dunbar earned cash at odd jobs while he searched for financial backers for the expensive copying machines he needed to lease in order to start College Copy Shop. Laurie, Brad and Gail Greenwood borrowed their money from the government and the bank, with their father co-signing their loans. Nancy Thomson and Joan Lavers had food and shelter provided by their husbands when they were getting started. Brian Brittain turned to his aunts to help finance the purchase of his first tranquility tank. Sharon James, Lynn Hubacheck, Nathan Zavier and Dianne Shore earned their first solo dollars on their own, doing what they do best.

Although Dianne Shore came from a less-than-affluent family, that didn't inhibit her. She now owns innumerable properties, including the whole southwest corner of Sherbourne and King Street East in Toronto, as well as the restaurant across the street. Her philosophy on money is: "Always be honest, and always pay back money borrowed as soon as possible. If you're short for whatever reason, be honest with your creditors; try to work out a reasonable pay-back arrangement even if you have to write hundreds of post-dated cheques for the rest of your life."

Mario Barocchi of Art World 700 Ltd. had enough money for one painting when he began as an art dealer at the age of sixteen on the streets of Milan, Italy. He sold one painting and bought two paintings and sold two paintings and bought four paintings. Today his holdings are enormous, and he is respected throughout the world.

The financing of your company can come from a number of sources: your own work, your family, your friends, your savings, bank loans, a variety of government (both federal and provincial) grants and loans and venture capital from the general public. There are positive and negative factors connected with each source.

All other factors being equal, the best money is the cheapest money.

Your Own Work: If you are starting a business that is not capital intensive, you may work at it part-time at first and expand as you gain customers and a reputation. This type of financing is possible in such areas as catering. It is also possible for plumbers and electricians and some home renovators who may already own their tools or equipment and who begin free-lancing jobs that eventually lead to a full-time income. It is also a probable means of financing for those in the creative arts such as writers, painters, designers and musicians.

Consider the advantages of this type of financing: you pay as you go, expanding only when you have the funds to do so, and you don't incur heavy obligations to others. The one disadvantage is that you may take longer to become established.

When George Prokos began the Public Relations Board of Canada, his previous experience was all he needed to capture lucrative accounts. Nathan Zavier and Lynn Hubacheck began Go Fer Enterprises at Christmas 1979. They both left their jobs one day and began their business the next, working for $10 an hour at free-lance assignments. Sharon James of Sharon's Catering started catering parties on a part-time basis, keeping her rent paid by working at jobs in local restaurants.

Many of the tycoons of yesterday thought nothing of free-lance and full-time work to build up the capital base for their enterprises. Like these men, Michael Gowling built his capital base by working free lance for three years in South America and Canada, performing a number of jobs before he set up his own production company.

Many husband-and-wife teams begin their businesses with one spouse working as a salaried employee while the other sets up the enterprise. The authors of this book took this route. One started the literary agency while the other continued to be employed by Coles Bookstores. When Coles was sold to Southam, Larry left and joined Authors' Marketing Services Ltd. as vice-president. He sold his Coles shares to Southam, and the proceeds were reinvested in the agency, therefore enhancing the new business and saving tax dollars as well. The money stayed in the family.

Eunice Webster's Apex Associates was created through work alone. Eunice put down a small deposit on a hotel room for her first seminar and paid her speaker a deposit. Then she proceeded to sell tickets knowing that the greater the number of sales, the greater the profit. She received cash for the tickets, and before she had to pay the remainder of the hotel bill and the speakers fee, the money was in her account. While living in California, Eunice had run a day care centre for children (during the time her own children were small). She rented a large house across the street from a school. She had to rent a house to live in anyway, so she chose one with a huge yard. Eunice had more than enough customers, each paying forty dollars per child per week, and Eunice's house became a profit centre.

Janet Rosenstock and Dennis Adair first founded their corporation Freelance Writing Associates, Inc. as a partnership. They began with two used manual typewriters and worked at home. They earned funds writing corporate brochures and educational materials, and as the money came in, it was reinvested in the business. Today, they write best-selling novels and take on other writing assignments.

If you are in a business that is not capital intensive, or doesn't need to be in its initial stages, your own work may finance you. If you can generate money on an ongoing basis, you can borrow later to expand or make shrewd investments.

Family: If you choose to borrow money from your family, do it in a businesslike way. It gives them a tax deduction, and it gives you a lower interest rate. But do not borrow from your family if you cannot stand the thought of doing so, or if guilt and pressure are going to be your interest payments. You don't want to be responsible for or listen to your grandmother saying, "Oh, Irving, you spent all of your grandfather's nest egg and now he needs an operation we can't pay for."

When you borrow from family, set up a repayment plan. Send them progress reports (these need not be formal) and make contracts as you would with a stranger.

Weigh the advantages of low or no interest rates and the disadvantages of possible guilt, antagonism and interference. Whether to go ahead is a personal choice, and it depends on the type of business you are going into, the amount of money you are borrowing and the type of family you have.

Borrowing from family is among the most traditional forms of financing. Family money has been invested in family businesses for centuries, and in some cultures it is still the sole means of building up family enterprises.

When Brian Brittain bought his first tranquility tank, he went to his aunt for money.

> I was extremely nervous when I went to borrow the money I needed. I just couldn't get up the courage to come right out and

> ask her for it. We talked about the weather; we talked about the family; we talked about everything but the reason I was there. Finally my aunt said to me, 'You need money, don't you?'
>
> I told her I did. I was willing to pay anything for her help. Without my saying another word, she agreed to lend me as much as I needed at ten per cent interest. The banks that turned me down would have demanded at least double that rate. I paid her back within six months, including the interest.

Mary Duncan, a specialist in document examination and forgery detection, did not need much money to start her business.

> To get my company started, other than years of education and training, all I needed was a magnifying glass, a good typewriter and membership in the Society of Graphoanalysis. I inherited some money from my father. My husband, who is a successful business man, backed me as well.

Another possible means of obtaining money from family members is to sell either shares in your firm or "points" on one or two items in your inventory. But speak to your lawyer about selling shares before you do so, since shareholders' rights vary with the type of incorporation you have, with the amount of investment and with the type of shares issued. By the same token, the investor's liability varies. An investor in an unincorporated venture is fully liable. The advantages are that your family member may profit by your success and that by offering shares you are competing with banks and the stock market for their attention.

Deal with your family as you would deal with anyone else. Stand by your agreements and do not run the risk of embarrassment or alienation. A final word of warning: money lent by family members who will make you eat crow for the rest of your life if you fail is not worth having.

Your Own Money: Opinion varies greatly on the advisability of using your own savings. Many soloists swear by using their own money because they feel they have greater control over their own businesses and because they derive pleasure and satisfaction from working toward their goal and seeing their money earn a profit.

Some other soloists agree with Albert Lowry who, in his recent book, *How to Become Financially Successful by Owning*

Your Own Business, suggests that using your own money leads to excessive and needless worry. Lowry feels that you will have enough on your mind in the beginning without worrying about becoming personally bankrupt.

There are ways to "use" your own money without actually using it, or by using only a portion of it. These will be discussed when we mention bank loans, but such "combination" financing does presuppose that you have some assets.

Using your own money tends to make you careful, and again, the less capital-intensive your business, the less the risk of investing your own funds.

Walter J. Schroeder of Dominion Bond Rating Service Ltd. describes his investment this way:

> The company was not capital-intensive. It was more labour-intensive and "good will" intensive. We didn't need much money to get it started, so I did not have to go to the banks. We had enough in the savings account, and my last employer presented me with a decent bonus when I left the firm.
>
> I preferred using my own money. When you use other people's money, not only do you pay interest on it, but you are also answerable to them. You have to provide them with information, and perhaps even give up ownership.
>
> There was a considerable amount of research into the company before we started, so when we made our projections we believed the company could turn around by the tail end of the first year. We were dead-on with our projections. We all believed that it would be the rip-roaring success that it was, and failure never crossed our minds.

Bank Financing: The amount you pay to a bank on the money you borrow depends on the following: how much of a risk the bank perceives you to be, whether or not your loan is secured, your reputation, your future earning power, and the record of your personal accounts and previous cash flow (i.e., the amount of money that passes through your account on a yearly basis).

Banks do take chances, but you pay through the nose if they have to take too much of a chance on you.

The most costly loan is an unsecured loan on a lump sum. Such a loan is much like a personal loan and will require a standard monthly repayment plus interest charges.

Next is a secured loan on a lump sum. This type of loan will also have monthly payments plus interest charges, but the interest will be lower because the loan is secured by an asset. Let us say you have $10,000 in term deposits that pay 15 per cent interest. If you use these as collateral for a secured loan of $10,000 at 17 per cent interest, your actual interest on borrowed money is 2 per cent. If your business fails, you will lose the portion of your own funds that is still outstanding on your loan. This form of financing is cheaper and less risky than actually cashing in your term deposits and using the money to set up the business.

The credit line is another form of loan. If you have a credit line based on your cash flow alone, your interest rate is higher than if you have a credit line based on an asset used as collateral. The advantage of the credit line is that your interest is charged at a daily rate rather than a pre-set rate, and you only pay for the actual amount of money you need. For example, if you own a $200,000 home, you set up a mortgage with the bank for a fraction of the home's value, say $30,000. The $30,000 becomes your credit line. The interest for this type of secured line of credit is usually the prime rate plus one per cent. If the bank prime rate (the rate given to the best customer) is 15 per cent, you pay 16 per cent, but your rate varies with the daily prime. If your credit line is $30,000, you may use only $10,000, and you only pay for $10,000. As money comes into your firm, your borrowed amount goes down; as you pay bills, it goes up. Thus, both the amount of your loan and the interest rate fluctuates.

The advantage of this type of initial financing is obvious. If you borrowed $30,000 as a lump sum, you would be tied to a yearly interest rate based on the rate the day you borrowed the money. You might borrow at 18 per cent and be committed to monthly payments plus 18 per cent even if the following month the interest rates fell to 12 per cent. Moreover, with a secured credit-line loan, your rate of indebtedness increases only on the day actual cheques pass through your account. The unsecured credit line (based on cash flow) has many of the same advantages, but the interest rate is higher.

It is also important to know that the interest rate on loans for your business is tax deductible.

It has been suggested that we have inherited an unhealthy

fear of banks because of the Great Depression. Banks called in loans, foreclosed on granny's farm and, according to some, were the cause of innumerable suicides.

Fred Bird had this unsettling fear whenever he entered a bank. For Fred, going to the bank to ask for money was "like going to traffic court, to appear in front of a judge who never smiles."

But bankers do smile. Whatever your personal fears, it is important to realize that banks are selling money, and they make money working with you and helping you to succeed. Your fears will be greatly eased if you do not overextend yourself and if you use only a portion of your assets as collateral.

Linda Kugelmass borrowed $7,500 to rent a store to sell her line of clothing, Carol Michard. Without borrowing the money she would not have been able to succeed. She would have barely been able to begin her solo journey. By working closely with her bank, however, her success became the bank's success and a good working relationship was born. Without the enabling functions of banks the creation of wealth would not and could not have occurred.

The bank is your professional colleague, and together you can both make money. So establish your account and take time to investigate the services your bank offers. Investigate the types of loans as well as investment certificates. Get to know your bank manager and the loans officers, and learn all the procedural details.

If your first act is to request financial assistance, you have to do your homework. According to Michael Gowling, those individuals who are turned down for loans to start their businesses are those whom the bank does not consider good managers. The bank simply does not believe that the individual can run a successful business. You need to be able to show that you know what you're doing. In order to accomplish this you need the lists suggested at the beginning of this chapter to prepare the following:

- a written description of your business.
- a projection of your cash flow for the first year, that is, how much money will pass through your account. This is not how much you will earn, but the gross amount that passes through your account.
- a profit and loss projection for the same period. To achieve this,

subtract liabilities from income. Include the payments on your proposed loan as well as the interest. Do not be unrealistic.
- a list of your assets.
- a description of your business experience and a summation of the "good will" you feel you have established.

In many cases an accountant should be consulted first. Accountants are trained to communicate with bankers, and you may wish to meet with an accountant before you go to the bank. If you are incorporated, you are required to have an accountant in any case. If you are not incorporated, you may already have someone to do your taxes. Accountants, like lawyers, specialize, so choose one who suits the needs of your business. You can find an accountant through friends or through professional organizations such as the Canadian Institute of Chartered Accountants. With your paperwork prepared, you are in a position to go to the bank to seek funds.

Fred Bird's first experience was a happy one.

> Finding the right bank manager was luck more than anything else. He just started managing the local bank which my wife and I used. My accountant was great in preparing all the paperwork and coaching me in the questions which might be asked and the ones I should ask.
>
> The bank manager was a young guy and curious about the photography business. I was nervous as hell. I had always worked in the creative end of the business and now I had to look and sound businesslike. He listened to my proposal and seemed to be impressed. He took one look at my client list, and almost fell off his chair.
>
> He said to me, 'Fred, you're dealing with nothing but A-1 clients: General Foods, Robin Hood, General Motors. There's nothing wrong with these kind of clients. It's different with stores; they're dealing with people off the street. Not you.'
>
> All I wanted was a line of credit from the bank to the tune of five thousand dollars. I got my line of credit. We were able to become friends. We could, in fact, go out for beer, and if he got on my nerves, I could call him whatever I liked.
>
> He's since moved to another branch, but I still use the same bank. I've also treated his replacements the same way.

As a chartered accountant, Michael Woods had a different experience.

> The banks like young professionals. We don't usually default on loans. If I ever went bankrupt, I would lose my C.A. certificate. That kind of motivation ensures that I keep my financial affairs in order.
>
> I just walked into the bank with no client base, no cash flow, nothing. They gave me twenty-five thousand dollars. There are times when I'm in a severe cash bind, but I never have any doubts that the situation will change for the better, and neither do the banks. As a professional, and as long as I have something on the ball, they will back me.

Not all encounters with a bank are as painless as those experienced by these two soloists. But it's worth noting that both claimed to be "lucky," a claim made by virtually everyone interviewed. They must be doing something right.

Sometimes, however, you can do all your paperwork correctly, but if the bank manager does not understand the type of business you're conducting, there may still be problelms. Remember, they are trained to deal with essentially average situations and can have some difficulty understanding new and different forms of business.

When Angus McKay and Andrew Crosbie began Ready Records, they did well locally, but decided it was time to grow and expand. Initially they were financed by funds from the family and what they earned at odd jobs.

> When we moved to Toronto, we transferred our London account to the local branch. At first there was no problem, but after a while when we started to need additional money, we ran into great difficulties. The manager of the local branch could not understand the recording industry.
>
> We spoke to some friends in our business, and they recommended their banker. The manager at their bank was young and had it all together and, most importantly, understood the industry. We still had to prepare the same paperwork and statements, but he understood our bottom line. It helped.
>
> We eventually worked out a good system with our manager. We try to alternate our visits so that one out of two visits is always good news. We land a good deal, and the first person to find out will be our bank manager. We try to treat him cordially as much as possible. It's important that he know us as human beings and not just two guys needing money.

William Sutton had to overcome much of his upbringing in order to approach the banks for money.

> My father was a tradesman. Built into his psyche was the belief that asking a bank for money is bad. It ain't bad! I've been working in public accounting and business for most of my life. Hell, all the banks are doing is selling money. It's no different than the person who is selling a car. Do you feel afraid when you approach a dealer to buy a car? Of course not! There's no reason to be afraid when you're asking to buy money. That's why they're there.
>
> We must finance our business at certain times of the year, and that's all there is to it. To do so requires borrowing. As much as I need space to work in, I need to borrow occasionally. You should not borrow indiscriminately, but if you have a viable business, you need money to open your doors; you need money to keep going until the business is able to earn enough on its own.
>
> I try to deal with a banker as if I'm buying a car. I shop around for the best price, and if I get it right off, fine. I'm not the type of guy who hammers and hammers until he gets that last ounce of flesh. I deal with my banker in a businesslike manner, and I'm not at all in awe of him. I'll take him out to dinner a few times a year or get him tickets for the hockey game. On those occasions, we'll talk about everything *except* business.
>
> I deal honestly with my banker at all times. In the first year I would always present him with quarterly reports on the state of my business, always feeling good when my projections were bang-on. Once the third-quarter numbers were not very good. I went to see him, showed him the figures, and said, 'There they are, and they're not very good. I need some more money.' He said, 'OK.' I also told him that I had around five thousand in plastic floating around town. He asked if that was all, and when I said yes, I got the money I needed. He appreciated my honesty, and he trusted me.
>
> I always keep my banker fully informed, although no more than is necessary. All he wants to know about is my base line, nothing more.

Kelly LaBrash did not need bank assistance in the initial financing of his company. The three original partners could cover virtually all of the day-to-day expenses. As the business grew and payrolls increased, it was necessary to establish a line of credit with their bank.

> We've always had a credit line, and our current line is close to five hundred thousand dollars. Our payroll can run as high as two hundred and fifty thousand dollars sometimes, and we pay almost one hundred thousand dollars every month in income tax. We'll bill our accounts every two weeks, and if they don't pay in four to six weeks, we wind up with a fairly large accounts receivable. As a result, we run on a continual credit line. Sometimes we get even, but usually we're running two to three hundred thousand in the hole. This is becoming a lot rougher with the current interest rates.
>
> In the beginning of our company, we had a line of credit with a particular bank. Receivables were slow in coming, and this bank was going to cut off our payroll. We did what anyone should do in the same situation—we changed banks.
>
> At first, we went to the bank with our hat in our hands. We needed them. Now they are coming to us because we have a good-sized account—eight million a year. We're not world beaters, but eight million dollars going through their books can pay the salary of a manager, an assistant manager and what not.
>
> The relationship with our new bank has worked out fine. In 1981 we had three fairly large contracts. We did the security work at the C.N.E. and the King Edward Hotel, and there was a large strike. Our credit line at that time was close to four hundred thousand dollars, and our payroll was close to a million bucks. We let our bank know that we would be exceeding our line of credit, and there was no problem. The bank will stick with you when they know that the business is there.

Taking in a Partner: One of the older forms of raising capital has been the partnership. The great merchant-trading companies of the middle ages were all partnerships, with each partner putting in a certain percentage of the starting venture capital and receiving a commensurate share of the profit.

There are a number of advantages to a financial partnership. Chief among the reasons cited by the soloists was that while they were business-oriented, their partner was the creative one, or vice versa. This depth of expertise can be crucial to a new company. Another major advantage is that when additional funds are required, the company can add more partners, only for a brief period if need be. Kelly LaBrash took such a tack early on in his business.

> The company was originally a partnership between myself and two others, Robertson and Andrews. Each of us was responsible for a different aspect of the company. Andrews left early for personal reasons, so Robertson and I bought him out, and remained equal partners until 1978.
>
> At that time, Robertson wanted to leave the business, so I took on a few more partners out of my share of the business, bought Robertson out and took on a few more partners on a temporary basis. By the end of 1979, I bought out the new partners, and retained eighty per cent control of the business. The other twenty per cent was held by a lawyer.

Michael Woods first went solo as a partner. His partnership arrangement lasted over three years and, like Kelly LaBrash's, ended amicably. For the last four years Michael has been operating independently. At the time of the interview, he wanted to go back into partnership.

> I need another partner if only to cover myself during holidays or when I'm sick. A well-run partnership of two, at the outset, can equal the income of a junior partner from a firm with ten or twenty people. Over time it will equal the income of a senior partner from that same mythical firm.

Fred Bird's experience with partners was somewhat different.

> Everybody has their own story about their partnership—how their partner was a bastard, a cheat and everything else. My former partner probably dislikes me as much as I dislike him. He was the business end of the company. I handled the creative end and made all the sales calls. I left all the paperwork and number shuffling up to him. I did not want to get involved in that because for me it was a real pain in the ass.
>
> In a short while the business started to fall apart. It was my doing to a large part because I couldn't get myself interested in the business end. We fought, and then ultimately ended the partnership. I suddenly had to learn about business. I had to learn how to keep records, pay the bills, and so on.

Venture Financing: In any major city you can find companies whose sole purpose is to invest in new companies. Their terms may seem far more harsh than those of a bank, but in certain respects they are taking fairly high risks which demand greater returns.

Occasionally, these companies will have an idea and hunt for the people who can execute their idea. Joanna Campion had her company financed in this way.

> It happened over dinner when a friend of my husband's was over. He was vice-president of a firm that specializes in financing other businesses. After dinner, I began talking to him about what was wrong with the company where I worked and how I would do a better job if I was president. He encouraged me to keep talking, and at the end of the evening, he asked me to work up a proposal for this company. If my proposal was as clear as my conversation, he would finance the company.
>
> Within a short time, they had agreed to the financing, and it worked out splendidly for me. They put up all the risk capital for office equipment, rent, salaries, including my own, as well as taking care of all the books and record keeping. For the first year or so, before the company got off the ground, it was an ideal set-up. There was so much to do, and it was a comfort to be bringing in a regular salary.
>
> I might have been able to arrange the financing through other sources, but the people at Helix Investments were there almost before the beginning. They believed in me and encouraged me. With minor exceptions it has worked out well for all of us. I'm able to devote my full-time to the running of the business. They take care of and worry about the financial end.

Strange as it sounds, Doug Dunbar could not, at first, get a penny from any bank to start his copying business. Among the reasons for his difficulty was that his business was brand new to Canada, and banks are somewhat reluctant to finance totally innovative ideas. Secondly, Doug was not from Toronto and had no track record or references. Toronto banks turned him down, so he went home to New Brunswick and spoke to the bankers he knew. They turned him down as well. If they lent him money and his business turned out to be a success, the revenue would only flow through a Toronto bank. It would not help the bank in New Brunswick.

> I returned to Toronto and moved into the old Ford Hotel. I worked evenings in the city and on weekends in the orchards outside of town to raise some money. During the day I would walk the streets of Toronto looking for someone to back my company.
>
> It took about six weeks of doing this before I found a group of people who were willing to lend me the two thousand five hundred dollars I needed to open my doors. Under the circumstances at the time, it was a fair agreement. They owned twenty-five per cent of the business now and in the future.
>
> The arrangement worked out well in the beginning, but I felt that it had to end. There was no incentive for me to build the business and expand. I had a meeting with these men, and they agreed to be bought out. A price was agreed, and they were paid by the end of the week.

Government Funding: The federal and/or provincial governments can be an excellent source of financing. Funding can be obtained through a number of programs they administer, and while the rates of interest charged by those programs are roughly the same as those charged by banks, the conditions under which they provide the funds are less stringent.

Each year the federal government publishes a booklet entitled *Assistance to Business in Canada*. This booklet may be obtained through the regional offices of the Federal Ministry of Industry, Trade and Commerce or through the Federal Business Development Bank (FBDB). The booklet lists and describes every program under federal jurisdiction, and there are hundreds. These programs range from basic seminars on how to start a business to incentives to certain key industries such as microtechnology or the resource industries of oil and gas. In between may be just the program that can help you.

Len Kubas of Kubas Research Consultants found such a program.

> We needed a word-processing machine. The savings in money and editorial time would make the machine worthwhile. My bank suggested that I purchase the machine from my credit line, but I couldn't do that. The credit line exists solely to carry me over periods when my cash flow has slowed down. It is not designed for the purchase of capital equipment. If I had listened to my bank, I would have had to withdraw sixteen

> thousand dollars of my twenty-thousand-dollar line of credit.
>
> I explored some other possibilities with my bank manager. We came across a program by which the Federal Business Development Bank would guarantee eighty per cent of any loan for the purchase of equipment. My bank processed the paperwork that same day, and the FBDB approved.
>
> The next morning, I had a loan for the purchase of the word processor. The upfront cost to me was only two thousand dollars, which I took against my credit line. That was much better than the sixteen thousand dollars I feared I would have to use.

In addition to the federal programs, there are many provincial government programs ranging from loans and grants to tax write-offs and tax credits. In matters of funding, government programs should not be overlooked.

To find out more about provincial programs, contact the ministry responsible for business and industry in your province.

Finding Government Aid, Information and (maybe) Financial Assistance

Federal

Department of Industry, Trade and Commerce,
235 Queen Street,
Ottawa, Ont. K1A 0H5
(613) 995-5771

Federal Business Development Bank,
901 Victoria Square,
Montreal, P.Q. H2Z 1R1
(614) 283-5904

The FBDB has five regional offices:
Atlantic: 1400 Cogswell Tower, Scotia Square, Halifax, N.S. B3J 2Z7
Quebec: 800 Victoria Square, Montreal, P.Q. H4Z 1C8
Ontario: 250 University Avenue, Toronto, Ont. M5H 3E5
Prairie and Northern: 161 Portage Avenue, Winnipeg, Man. R3B 0Y4

B.C. and Yukon: 900 W. Hastings Street, Vancouver, B.C. V6C 1E7

Alberta

Department of Economic Development,
12th Floor, Pacific Plaza,
10909 Jasper Avenue,
Edmonton, Alberta T5J 3M8
(403) 427-0669

British Columbia

Ministry of Industry and Small Business Development,
Parliament Building,
Victoria, B.C. V8V 1X4
(604) 387-6701

Manitoba

Department of Economic Development and Tourism,
358 Legislative Building,
Winnipeg, Manitoba R3C 0V8
(204) 944-2036

New Brunswick

Department of Finance,
Centennial Building,
Fredericton, N.B. E3B 5H1
(506) 453-2511

Newfoundland

Department of Development,
Box 4750,
St. John's, Nfld. A1C 5T7
(709) 737-2781

Nova Scotia

Department of Development,
Box 519,
Halifax, N.S. B3J 2R7
(902) 424-8920

Ontario

Ministry of Industry and Tourism,
900 Bay Street, Hearst Block,
Queen's Park,
Toronto, Ont. M7A 1T2
(416) 965-7075

Prince Edward Island

Department of Tourism, Industry and Energy,
Box 2000,
Charlottetown, P.E.I. C1A 7N8
(902) 892-7411

Quebec

Department of Industry, Trade and Tourism,
1, Place Ville-Marie, 23rd Floor,
Montreal, P.Q. H3B 3M6
(418) 643-5084

Saskatchewan

Department of Industry and Commerce,
3rd Floor, 2121 Saskatchewan Drive,
Regina, Sask. S4P 3V7
(306) 565-2226

Chapter 9

Accounting I

Regardless of the method you choose to obtain financing for your company, and regardless of whether or not you are incorporated, you should adhere to strict methods of reporting and analyzing your firm. It is surprising to discover that very few soloists have even a beginner's knowledge of bookkeeping. It is suggested by many that since inadequate bookkeeping is a symptom of bad management, this lack of knowledge is directly related to many business failures. Without proper costing procedures and constant monitoring, a great idea can become worthless. So it is essential for the soloist to obtain a rudimentary understanding of basic accounting procedures.

When we first started our company, our accountant surmised (from the pile of shoe boxes and the match covers inside that contained our financial records) that we knew nothing about bookkeeping.

After pouring through some of the boxes, he came to the conclusion that we needed an immediate crash course in what he called *Accounting I.* With some long green sheets, some sharpened pencils and our shoe box marked "April," his assistant took us into another room and locked the door.

This chapter is relatively short because it cannot cover the myriad of information on accounting. There are many specialized books on the subject that will take you step by step through the process and you can learn best by doing. If you have an accountant, you will be shown exactly how to keep the books.

Rule 1. *Always keep all your receipts.* There are firms that specialize in reasonable systems to help organize you. One of these is Daytimers which provides little books and files for each month.

Rule 2. Purchase accountant's sheets (12 column) or a book. Ask your accountant which he prefers. The book is called a ledger, and ledgers come with different numbers of columns.

Rule 3. Ask for instructions based on your first month of operation.

Rule 4. Have your accountant check your work after the first month.

Every bit of income and every expense is called a "transaction," and all transactions have to be recorded and placed in the appropriate column. The columns represent nothing more than vertical files which enable you and your accountant to see how much was earned from various endeavours and how much was spent on various categories. Why not just list earnings and expenditures, you ask? Well, because certain categories of expenses are tax deductible. Also, some areas of your business may earn more than others and you want to know what is profitable and what is not.

The accounting system most widely used in called *double entry accounting*. This means that every transaction is recorded in two or more accounts with equal debits and credits. Confused? Follow these simple steps:

Mark the first page of your ledger *Fees Journal.*

- Label the first column *Accounts Receivable*. Every penny you receive is entered in this column.
- Indicate in the remaining columns where the money comes from.

Fees Journal

May 1-May 31	Accounts Receivable	Sales	Advance	Installations
Acme Grime, Inc.	$200.	$200.		
Fred's	$125.		$125.	
Acme Grime, Inc.	$150.			$150.
Total	$475.	$200.	$125.	$150.

If you total the Sales, Advances and Installation columns, it equals the amount of money in the first column which is the receivables column. This is double entry accounting.

Now skip a few pages in your ledger and begin a new account. Label this page *Cash Receipts*.

- Write in the first column, *Bank*; the second column, *Accounts Receivable*; the next column, *Bank Loan* (if you have one); and the next, *Shareholder's Account*. If your corporation is composed of more than yourself, you will require a column for each of the other principles from whom money will be transferred. Now on this page we have all the money received.

Cash Receipts

May 1-June 1	Bank	Accounts Receivable	Bank Loan	Shareholder's Account
Transfer to Corporation	$2,000.			$2,000.
Acme Grime	$200.	$200.		
Fred's	$125.	$125.		
Acme Grime	$150.	$150.		
Bank Loan	$15,000.		$15,000	

As before, the totals of the other columns equal the first column.

No, this is still not the end. Skip a few more pages and open a new account. Label this page *Banking and Transactions*.

- Mark the first column *Bank*. This is for outgoing money. Write down to whom any cheque was made out. Do not write down what it was for; this is what the other columns are for. As a beginning soloist you will have more on this page than on the others.
- Column 2 will be labelled *Bank Charges*. (Bank charges exist with or without a loan. Cheques cost money.)
- Label the third column *Legal, Accounting and Bookkeeping Fees*. Yes, you can pay yourself or a member of your family to do the books.
- Mark in column 4, *Rent*.
- The remaining columns will be labelled with the words that indicate your expense breakdown. They will include such categories as phone, transportation, entertainment, business equipment, office supplies, salaries or occasional labour and loans to

shareholders (this is money you take out of the corporation).

Again, the total of columns 2 through 12 will total the same as column 1 which includes all your bank transactions in terms of withdrawals. The Fees Journal, Cash Receipts Journal and Banking and Transactions Journal will all cross-check one another. Different accountants may have slightly different titles for your pages, and certainly the labels on your columns will vary since they are dictated by the nature of your business.

This is not as complicated as this simplified explanation makes it sound. It enables you to take full advantage of the tax structure, and it tells you where and how you are spending money.

Mastery of Accounting I enables you to go on to the next step: projections.

Some people are bubbly and enthusiastic. So much so that they initially make wildly optimistic projections that put their future income somewhere near the present income of Conrad Black. Others are bleakly conservative and are recognizable by the frowns on their faces. The first type announces near millionaire status by the end of three months. The second feels he might break even in five years. Somewhere between these extremes is the individual who is realistic and combines realism with enthusiasm and faith in self.

Projections include three elements: 1. the reality of your account books; 2. realistic growth potential; and 3. a consideration of inflation. Who can forget the old joke about the man who is in a coma for a hundred years and wakes up overjoyed at the thought of how the $10,000 he invested a hundred years ago had grown. "I have a million dollars!" he shouts, overjoyed. He goes to the phone to call his bank, and the operator says, "Please deposit one million dollars."

Realistically, you may expect your income to increase by 25 per cent the first year, but if the inflation rate is 12 per cent, your real income increase will only be 13 per cent because your expenses will increase with your income. The total optimist will think only of total income and tend to forget the amount to be paid off in loans, the funds that belong to those who have bought shares and the rising costs that may be incurred as a result of worldwide inflation. To make realistic projections, you must consider the length of time it will take to collect monies owed, the full expense of paying off loans, the inflation rate and other factors of importance. Success is more than one lucrative sale. The trick is to remain committed, enthusiastic and contented while maintaining a certain caution.

The first time we seriously attempted to do our cash-flow projections, we thought we would have to move to a tax haven because of the millions we would make. We were certain that every item we offered would sell at the highest possible price. Didn't Judith Krantz receive over three million dollars for just one book?

Fortunately, we hesitated before purchasing tickets. We were still waiting for our gusher six months later. Negotiations were not as rapid in some cases as we had anticipated, and the final price in the negotiations was well below what we had hoped for (though sometimes we received more than expected on some individual books). And to our total shock and surprise, some of our product did not sell at any price. When cheques were due we were certain a train had been derailed or a plane had crashed. It is a rule that bills always arrive on time, but payments are always late.

Chastened by experience, we prepared another cash-flow projection. This is known as the journey from manic to depressive. Enthusiasm was replaced with overcompensated conservatism. If one of us won the lottery, there might be groceries in the house. Assuming, of course, that we could afford a lottery ticket.

Trying once again, we utilized all we had learned from experience. The cycle of our business seemed more apparent, and understanding the cycle helped us to make a more accurate projection. With several contracts in hand, we knew when certain sums should be arriving (mail strikes and train derailments notwithstanding). The consulting function of our business was becoming more regular, and the number of clients was more predictable. In addition, we had refined our knowledge of the people we represented and could reasonably anticipate the sale of certain items within a fairly defined price range. Implicit in our cash-flow forecast was our belief that if most of what we were planning came to fruition, it would equal a specific sum of money.

Six months later, we were delighted to note that our projections were off by only 8 per cent, and that figure would be lowered when a cheque we knew to be in the mail arrived.

An accurate cash-flow projection allows for realistic planning. It gives you a reasonably realistic idea of the financing you will need and indeed of the kind of financing you should seek.

You should know what you and your family need to live on and finance accordingly. Underfinancing can be extremely dangerous. It is not impossible to "scale down" one's standard of living, but it is difficult and requires the co-operation of all family members. Thus, there are two areas to consider: the business area which can suffer immensely when underfinanced, and the personal area which can cause frustration when underfinanced. No one wants to work and work and not be able to afford the occasional film, dinner out or family vacation. Leisure-time activities cost money, but they are often the reward we seek for hard work, and indeed, they are the reward we have earned. Cutting your budget to the bare bones will result in personal unhappiness, and the soloist needs personal contentment to make a success of his or her business.

But there are ways to hold the financial line and as a beginning soloist you should consider each expense. Without underfinancing your business, you can still expand slowly. The following are items you should consider.

A secretary: Does your business really require a secretary or can you or members of your family perform the functions just as well? Would it be more reasonable over the long haul to invest in a "smart typewriter" for business letters if large numbers of such letters are necessary? Some of the new "smart typewriters" work with tape recorders. They have three-page memories. You type only the heading on your form letter, and the typewriter will type individual copies at fast speed. Your correspondence is stored on the tape. The cost of such typewriters is $3,000 to $4,000. The cost of a secretary is upward from $12,500 a year plus employee benefits and the added expenses incurred in bookkeeping. A word processor, which does much more than a smart typewriter, can run from $9,000 to around $20,000 with many available in the $15,000 bracket. A home computer with a printer for word processing can run anywhere from $12,000 to $30,000 with several adequate ones at the bottom end of the price scale.

Whether or not you require a secretary or a machine that does the work of a secretary depends on the nature of your business.

In addition, one government youth-employment program provides half the salary for part-time student help. Such programs should be investigated. See your local Manpower Office for information.

A clerk: Can members of your family help out? Can you hire part-time student labour? Estimate the number of hours of help you need, and hire accordingly. You may only require additional help during peak hours if you are running a retail business. Can your family help during these hours or can you get by with part-time student help? The minimum wage is less for those under eighteen, and there are many responsible sixteen- and seventeen-year-olds, seeking ten to fifteen hours' employment a week.

A car: How essential is an automobile to your business? To your family? Obviously, many kinds of solo endeavours require an automobile. Others do not. A car may be a necessity, but for many it is an expensive luxury.

A car may cost $9,000. A pick-up truck which is often more useful for the soloist who has to transport materials may be cheaper. The insurance may be in the $450 range if you have a decent driving record (insurance rates are up for new cars). The cost of parking depends on whether or not you have parking accommodation and how often you pay for parking on your travels. But let's estimate it at $400 a year. How much gas you use depends on how much you drive. If you drive 16,000 kilometres a year and get 10 kilometres to the litre, your gasoline costs will be over $600 a year. Your maintenance costs will run $300 a year on a new vehicle. The total cost is then $4,750 per year, including the cost of your vehicle pro-rated over three years. There are obvious ways to lower this figure, but if you live in an area where you can get along without a car, and if you do not require a car for your business, you can eliminate this expense altogether.

An office: Can you work from your home? Is there a room that can be converted to an office? The answer to this question again depends on the type of business you are in. Clearly if you require a large workshop or warehouse space, this is not a solution. You can, of course, combine an office with workshop or warehouse, and the closer you live to where you work, the more reasonable your transportation costs.

Office decorations: You do not require decorator colours or touch-tone telephones. Be frugal and impress your clients with the fact that you pass on the savings to them. Low overhead means more reasonable terms and higher profits.

Corporate Charge Cards: These *can* be useful for accounting purposes, but they are dangerous for the undisciplined and costly as well. You can pay cash and get a receipt. Even parking lots give receipts. Revolving charge accounts, which include all bank cards, and many other credit cards charge interest on interest, since your interest becomes part of your total bill on which your monthly payment is based. If you maintain a revolving balance of $1,000 on a charge card for one year, you pay more than twice as much in interest as you would to a bank on an outright loan for the same amount.

Office supplies: Try to buy in quantity. Many firms maintain "cash and carry" stores and give a generous discount to the customer who picks up his or her own purchases from the warehouse. If this is possible, do it.

This list is by no means complete. It can't be because the needs of individual businesses vary and so do the items that can be scrimped on. Being frugal in certain areas of your business expenses is not the same as underfinancing. Spending $1,500 on an electronic typewriter and not being able to afford ribbons is underfinancing. Buying cloth ribbons (which last longer) instead of carbon ribbons is frugality.

Insurance: Even if you are incorporated, you must consider insurance. First, your bank loans ought to be insured so that in the event of your death, your family is not left in debt. Second, if you have purchased valuable assets (office equipment, computers, supplies, etc.), these should be insured against loss. Replacing them in case of theft is an avoidable expense.

Service Contracts: If you have machinery or technological devices (such as a computer or word processor), you may be asked to purchase a service contract. Such contracts do save money, but they are costly. Do not purchase a service contract on any item till the warranty expires. And before you purchase any service contract, find out the probable costs of repair and maintenance visits.

Ask yourself the following questions:

1. Do I need this item? List the reasons why you need it.
2. Do I need to hire personnel? Make a list of the chores hired personnel have to perform. Estimate the number of exact working hours they are needed. Cut where you can.
3. Is "image" important to the success of my business?
4. Can I get along without a personal or business vehicle? Or, can I purchase a small pick-up truck and a cover for it, thereby making it useful as a business and family vehicle?

Accounting I is more than a lesson on how to keep the books. It involves thinking out your potential income and keeping your initial costs down to a reasonable level.

Remember the old adage, "a penny saved is a penny earned"? It still applies.

Chapter 10
Getting Paid

Many people believe that the basic difference between success and failure in business is the intelligence of the individual soloist. *Wrong*! The difference lies in the ability to get paid. In order to keep your business thriving you have to master the art of collecting what is owed you.

You may create the world's greatest mousetrap. You may establish a dynamite distribution network and sell millions of mousetraps. Mice around the world may live in dread, fearing that your creation is soon to appear outside their dwellings. But while you are conquering the world's mice, you will have bills to pay, salaries to meet, daily overhead expenses to cover, all to come from money you are owed. If you fail to collect, your business will fail.

As many soloists before you have discovered, it is emotionally difficult to demand payment. Part of the difficulty comes from the fact that soloists are usually engaged in work they love and in the early stages sometimes feel guilty about getting paid for doing what they enjoy so much.

Fred Bird had to force himself to call his customers, at times spending two hours building up the courage. After six years in business, Michael Woods still hates to press delinquent or bad accounts. But Mary Duncan chose to take an account to small claims court to get paid, and Marlys Carruthers is prepping herself for a court appearance too.

You would do well to learn a lesson from the folks at the phone company. They know how to run their accounts receivable department. They never hesitate to remind you of an overdue bill, and they have no compunction about discontinuing your service. This is one of the reasons why Bell is a sound investment.

All *your* creditors demand payment; why should you be different? You do not have to assume the personality of a snarling collection agency, but you have to deal with monies owed to you in a businesslike way.

It is important, especially in the beginning, to give some serious thought to the ways in which you will handle bills. Here are some questions that ought to be asked:

1. Are your bills clear? Do you put a *date payable* on your bills, or do you specifiy *thirty days, sixty days or ninety days*?
2. Are you in a position to offer a discount for prompt payment?
3. Can you operate a "cash and carry" business?
4. What are your options for collecting?

The Retail Trade

Retailing can be one of the most hazardous forms of soloing. You normally pay for your stock on a thirty-, sixty- or ninety-day basis. But *you are paid* for your stock as it is sold. And you must also consider what is known in the retail trade as "shrinkage"—the term applies to items shoplifted ("the five-finger discount"), items vandalized in the store (be it clothing torn or stained, or melons squeezed too hard), and items otherwise spoiled or damaged. The amount of shrinkage depends on what you are selling, but the percentage is high and growing higher.

Shrinkage must be considered when you set the prices for the items you sell. Some damaged goods can be sold at a discount, but those which are out and out stolen are a dead loss. Is this a big loss to retailers? You bet. It is estimated that the cost of shoplifting to retailers in Canada is one million dollars a day. In addition to shoplifting, there are losses incurred through bad cheques, bad credit cards and even counterfeit money. Recently, for example, there was a rash of phony American fifty-dollar bills in circulation.

Retailers are paid in three different ways: cash, credit cards and cheques.

Cash: In many ways this is the safest way for the retailer to be paid. But there are cautionary measures that should be taken. The first is to beware of large bills. The second is for the retailer and his or her staff to stay in touch with police bulletins on the denomination of counterfeit bills making the rounds. (This is a special problem in Canada because U.S. money is readily accepted, though in the

United States it is extremely difficult to get retailers to take Canadian funds.) The retailer must be cautious of American bills.

Credit Cards: Retailers pay anywhere from 3 to 5 per cent for the pleasure of accepting credit cards, the actual amount depending on the gross of the specific business. Credit cards do have specific advantages. Even if the credit card is bad, the retailer gets his money as long as he has taken the proper precaution of checking on sales over $50. Since more and more consumers are shopping with plastic, the retailer who refuses to accept credit cards is denying himself access to a major segment of the market.

Cheques: Cheques can be risky, though certain precautions can be taken. Some retail stores (grocery stores for example) issue cheque-cashing identification cards, and in some areas there are cheque-verification systems available to retailers. The retailer pays for cheque verifications made through a central computer. These are widely used in the United States and are spreading to Canada. A retailer who accepts cheques should always insist on adequate identification. Passing a bad cheque or writing a cheque on an account in which there is no money is an offense, but this seldom helps the retailer who has been taken.

Retailers should be very wary of offering discounts. Discounting is a tried and true practice, but it ought to be applied only to prompt payments. Joan Lavers encountered a problem common to many retailers when she decided to allow special discounts to friends and family. While special prices every now and then for "special customers" is considerate and thoughtful, Joan had to severely curtail the practice.

> I began running the risk of turning What's Cooking? into an exclusive wholesale business for all my friends. It had to stop. When the business first started, the cash-flow projections were determined by a full markup on sales. By selling my merchandise at wholesale prices, I wasn't even coverng my overheads.

Doug Dunbar has always taken a frugal and conservative approach to money, believing that you should never spend more than you have, and you should spend only when you can afford it.

We do not accept any charge cards, we discourage charge accounts, and we do not pickup or deliver. This helps to keep our costs down.

I've always operated, both in business and personally, on the principle of keeping everything simple. In other copying shops, there are extra charges for legal-size paper, colour stocks, three-hole punch paper and collating. This has never been our policy. Our prices are openly displayed, and there are no hidden costs. A customer, even with a minimal intelligence, should not be surprised by the bill.

A further advantage of operating on a cash basis is that I'm able to pay my bills immediately. A shipment of paper can arrive, and even if I have thirty days to pay, I'll make out a cheque on the spot. I don't think I get any preferential treatment from my suppliers for doing this, but we are treated well by them.

We now have quite a pile of money stashed away. It's with a broker, and we keep it in the money markets on a thirty-day basis. It's been accumulating now for two or three years.

Sam Blyth runs his tour business in much the same manner—strictly "cash and carry." Before being booked on one of Sam's extraordinarily exotic tours, the customer has to leave a deposit of several hundred dollars. No deposit, no booking. Once the booking is confirmed, the customer must pay the full amount in advance. In the event of non-payment, the tour is cancelled and a percentage of the deposit is retained (depending on when the cancellation dates are specified in the contract and whether or not the customer has cancellation insurance). The advances and the percentage of deposits that may be retained are controlled by the travel industry and the government for the benefit of both customers and travel agents. Fly now and pay later is a fine principal only for the travel agent who wants to end up being owed large sums of money.

Nancy Thomson and Eunice Webster get paid upfront as well, eliminating all the needless paperwork of following up on invoices. To enroll in one of Nancy Thomson's eight-week courses, you must pay in advance either by cheque or credit card. Nancy is thus assured of being able to pay salaries and expenses before her courses begin. And without paying Eunice Webster in advance for her tickets to seminars, you won't get in.

A firm policy decision at the beginning on how you get paid can save innumerable headaches over money worries. Be clear about your fee schedule so that your accounts know accurately how much and when they are expected to pay.

But realize that there are times when you will have to press collections. If payment is expected in thirty days, you want it in thirty days, not in sixty, ninety or one hundred and twenty. And, if you can help it, don't fall into the trap of having highly profitable long-term potential and a current cash-flow crunch (though in some businesses, this is unavoidable, especially initially).

Don't let your business die through reluctance to ask for what was rightfully yours.

Michael Woods was honest when he related:

> It's a real pain in the ass to have people owing me money, and still I have to go to the bank and borrow an additional thousand dollars. If these deadbeats paid me what was owed, I'd be sitting plush.
>
> It was hard in the beginning to press people for payment. I'm not selling a pack of cigarettes, I'm selling myself, something intangible. How do I put a value on that? The first time I had to ask people for money, I was riddled with these self-doubts. [I would ask:] Am I really worth what I'm charging this poor guy?
>
> It took much soul-searching to make that first call, and I still don't like doing it. Now I've resolved in my mind that the bills I send out are eminently reasonable, and they should be paid. For the first few years, it was really tough. I would always wonder if I pressed the guy too hard would I lose him as a client. Would I create bad will?
>
> I consciously reached the conclusion that people expect that they are going to have to pay the bill. So when I call them up and ask when they're going to pay, there's no sweat off anyone's nose, and it doesn't affect the interpersonal relationship at all. After sixty or ninety days, I find that a simple phone call, not at all threatening, is generally enough. I'll either get the cheque or a series of post-dated cheques.

Fred Bird had a hard time acquiring the knack of getting paid.

> The one thing I don't like about being in business for myself is that good-guy/bad-guy routine. You're a good guy to the

creative people, and they give you assignments. But then you must be a bad guy to the accounting people, because they just want to sit on your bill. I'm usually dealing with large corporations, and my two-thousand-dollar bill is peanuts to them, really peanuts. The accountant there figures if he can sit on my bill for ninety days, well that's two thousand less they have to borrow or two thousand more they can collect interest on for ninety days.

One time when I was strapped for cash and my credit line was just about exhausted, I had to phone up some clients and ask to be paid. I must have sat around for about two hours figuring out everything they would say, and how I would counter it . . . Finally, I made up my mind and said, 'I'm going to do it right now!' It was scary, but they were all as nice as they could be and they paid.

Lately I started charging interest on unpaid accounts. The banks do it, and everybody else is doing it. I was a little afraid in the beginning. What if the client said, 'Go screw yourself'? But nobody said that.

William Sutton has the ultimate sanction at his disposal, yet he carefully assesses the long-range advantages of patience and accommodation and weighs those factors against short-term needs.

Our problems with payments are no different than any other business. Now especially, people are trying to hold on to their money as long as they can. In the sports business, there are a number of franchises that are in trouble from time to time, and it is more difficult to collect from them.

If they don't pay, we do have something to take away. We simply cancel the policy. The trick though is knowing when to use that hammer. At times it will pay to hold off, say, for a month. The guy will remember that you were reasonable and will come to you with more business. When we decide that someone is using us, we just call him up and tell him that he has fifteen days to get us a cheque or it's all over.

The attitudes expressed by both William Sutton and Michael Woods are excellent examples of the long view. As they both intend to remain in business, they are actively building up a reservoir of good will by not being unnecessarily harsh with customers who are slow to pay. This is a business proposition. The soloist has to weigh different factors.

On the surface, it may seem that a soloist might be better off without the foot-dragging type of account. Nevertheless, we all run into periods when paying our bills is difficult. One solution to this problem is to arrange a payment schedule, taking a little at a time so that you can ease your cash-flow problems while accommodating those of your customer. But do not hesitate to call the tardy customer and ask why payment has not been made.

Establishing Your Worth

Soloists who perform a service (as opposed to those who sell an item) have a problem—they are selling not only a service, but themselves.

When you initiate your business, you have to establish your worth on the open market. To your mother, you may be worth a million dollars, but what are you worth to others? If you are offering a service that is readily offered by other people or organizations, the price you charge must be competitive. In some solo professions, fees are established by professional associations, but in many it's a matter of competition combined with reputation. Herein lies an important point—your value changes with your reputation.

Establishing your worth is simple in the beginning. If you are a carpenter, you survey the fees charged by other carpenters to find "the going rate." But as you become known as a fine craftsman, your rate increases. You may also increase your fees as inflation demands or as you become more aware of your own value. You may end up spending half the time you once did "consulting," yet reap twice the money you did in the beginning for that part of the job.

No reputable business person fails to be open about fees. Discuss what you charge with your customers and make clear the terms of payment. This saves hassles later.

Mary Duncan, the document examiner, related:

> I usually get paid after a case and promptness of payment depends, in part, on the lawyer being paid promptly. Gen-

> erally, I will send a statement to the lawyer who hired me. He can, if he so chooses, maintain that he has not yet been paid by the client, although they usually get my fee before they get their own, and they are able to pay me quickly.
>
> In a number of cases, it may take anywhere from a few months to a few years before the work I do appears in court. I'm always paid as soon as my work is submitted. If I have to appear in court as an expert witness, the lawyer is once again billed but only for my time.
>
> I didn't have much difficulty establishing a fair fee for myself for court appearances; it's roughly comparable to that of a lawyer. When you consider the amount of responsibility involved—after all, when I am in court many of the best lawyers in the country are cross-examining me—my fee seems fair. Their job is to destroy me and my credibility as an expert witness. Now that I have reached a point where my credibility is high and my opinions are respected, I don't consider my fee high.

To establish your worth, find out what others in the same field are being paid. If there is no one in the same field, you will have to test the waters and see what you can charge. Assess yourself realistically. If you are working for corporations as a free lancer, consider what it would cost them to keep someone with your talent on the payroll. Think about the value of your creativity if you are in a creative field. Value your education and experience. If you have spent many years gaining the education and experience to do a specific job, build that education and experience into your hourly charges.

And when you have decided on your fee schedule, do not hesitate to set terms for payment. Enforce those terms unless it benefits *you* to be lenient.

Tips for Getting Paid

1. If you are in a service field, ask for money to bind the contract, a portion of the fee on completion of the service and the remainder within a specified period of time.
2. Insist on cash where applicable.

3. If you take credit cards, take into consideration the cost of using them. If you take cheques, insist on proper identification.
4. Avoid excessive discounting to family and friends.
5. Take deposits and arrange payments in thirds to facilitate cash flow.
6. Establish a rapport with law enforcement agencies and obtain information from them on bogus bills and recent scams and fraud.
7. Always let your clients know your fees in advance. People hate surprises.
8. Insist upon a retainer or advance.
9. Issue reminders if you are not paid when your contract specifies you will be.
10. If you are not paid when the contract specifies, begin with a phone call to the client. The first call should be polite—a friendly reminder. After ten days, ask if the client has financial difficulties and either arrange a payment schedule (post-dated cheques) or ask when payment can be anticipated.

If the client refuses to pay, you have the following options:

- Write off the account. In this case you will want to weigh the amount owed against the cost of collecting it.
- Take partial payment. Again, weigh the amount owed against the cost of collecting the full amount.
- Sell the account to a collection agency. Their fees vary, so investigate this line of action. And be aware that you don't get paid until they are paid. Normally, they take a percentage of the face value of the amount owed.
- If the amount is under a certain amount (which varies from province to province), you may be able to go to small claims court. But a judgement against your client still does not guarantee that you will be paid. The judgement has to be enforced. All that usually occurs is that your client's credit rating is affected.

Several of these options will probably result in the loss of the account.

For those in retailing, there are added cautions that might better be expressed under the heading "keeping your money." These include all possible measures against "shrinkage." Price your merchandise clearly so that price tags cannot be switched. Maintain overhead mirrors for spotting shoplifters, maintain tight security and never keep cash in your store (or in your home) overnight. If your deposit is large, arrange for an escort to the bank, and if you regularly have large deposits, there are firms that specialize in delivering them to banks.

Again, knowing your worth and getting paid are essential to the soloist. *Don't hesitate* to ask for money you have earned.

Chapter 11

Building Your Business

To be successful, a business must grow. The nature and speed of growth depends on you, on the nature of your business and on the market.

One fundamental point to keep in mind is that your best chance for success is what might be called the insurance of diversified accounts. Many beginning soloists are lulled into partial inertia when they obtain one large account. This account is seen to be so big that it offers security for life. But if the account dries up for any one of a hundred reasons, the soloist is devastated. Diversity is the key to success.

The Account Base

No matter what type of business you are in, nothing will happen until you are able to generate business, and generating business comes from establishing, then expanding, an account base.

An account is simply an individual or a company with whom you establish a working relationship. You are paid for a product or a service. If you are in a retail business, your account base consists of the customers who come into your store. If you sell placemats with horoscopes on them, your accounts are the restaurants who buy your placemats. If you are a masseuse, your accounts are the tired, weary people who seek your services.

Nathan Zavier and Lynn Hubacheck built their account base from scratch. They aggressively sought out jobs that needed to be done and expressed their willingness to perform the jobs. By providing good service to those individuals, they established long-term accounts.

When Marlys Carruthers, Joyce Krusky and Lynn McLaughlin began selling their cookbook, *Good to the Last Bite*, they built their account base by developing a selling product and then meeting people. All three women are quite personable, and the book buyers they sold to became long-term accounts. Even though the three friends knew little about publishing and marketing, they knew enough to sell their $12.95 cookbook for $8 wholesale. The differential meant that the buyers for book chains and individual stores could make money themselves. The three women further assisted buyers by backing up their book with strong and effective promotion. They advertised widely and tried to appear on almost every radio and television talk-show. Their success brought success to those who stocked it and insured the three of further orders and co-operation on their next venture. They are now in the planning stages for their next book, confident that they can repeat their success.

These examples point up the fact that to have an account base, clients must come back again and again. And they will only give you their business again if they are satisfied customers.

Accounts are the building blocks of your enterprise. George Prokos of the Public Relations Board of Canada builds accounts by providing excellent public relations. People come back to him because success and steady business depends on how many articles he can place in the media. George is good at his job. Returning clients insure his future and enable him to continue to run a thriving business.

It may seem elementary to remind soloists that accounts are built on either a fine product or on dependable service, but it is an element that is often forgotten. Joan Lavers tells the story of the advertising writer she once hired who couldn't write. After the embarrassment of sending out a brochure that was grammatically incorrect, Joan was further faced with the problem of ridding herself of the soloist when he showed up for additional work.

Do the job well. Do it on time.

When you pay for a product or service, you are making an investment. When Michael Woods is hired as an accountant, his clients expect him to save them money. They respect his financial advice. No one would keep an accountant if their investment in his fees did not justify the payment made.

Sharon James of Sharon's Catering is dealing in other people's investments too. When her clients have a party, they're investing their money in delighting their guests with good food and service. If Sharon's presentation is below par, the customer does not receive his or her money's worth. It is the high quality of Sharon's preparations that keep her customers coming back and recommending her to their friends.

Developing Your Account Base

When Bruce and Vicki Lansky of Meadowbrook Press sold their first book, *Feed Me, I'm Yours!*, they developed their account base by proving their babyfood cookbook would sell. They put the books into stores on a consignment basis and included free-standing display units as well. They sold hundreds of thousands of copies of their book by proving the book's value to the retail book buyers.

The most important word in the soloist's vocabulary is perseverence. To do that, they had to overcome a lot of resistance, to persevere despite skepticism and disbelief. *I-Ching*, the ancient book of Chinese wisdom, uses the phrase "perseverence furthers." To succeed and to build your business, you must persevere. Disappointment, frustration and rejection can occur. For the first four years Sandy Simpson ate at her parents home every weekend; otherwise she wouldn't have had anything to eat. By her own admission, her bank account was a joke, but she persevered. It took Sandy a full four years for her art gallery to start paying, but the work she now does and the rewards she receives have made her perseverance through hard times worth her initial effort and sacrifice.

Audrey Grant spent many nights looking at empty bridge tables in her club, at unopened packs of cards and at pencils that still retained their sharpened points. But she never doubted for a moment that eventually the tables would be crammed, cards would be thrown away from overuse, and there would be a huge demand for newly sharpened pencils. It took almost two years of persistent building of her club to reach a level that was satisfactory.

Audrey never gave up. She never conceded defeat or ruin. She persevered.

The Five W's

Obtaining accounts and expanding the number of accounts you

bring with you begins when you let the world know you are open for business. Let potential customers know the five W's:

- Who you are
- What you are selling
- When you are open
- Where you are located
- Why your product or service fills a need

Begin to spread the word about your business before your doors even open. Expand your contacts by every means available (more about that in the next chapter). Join clubs, arrange for advertising, tell your friends to spread the word about you, put up posters announcing your opening and explain your functions. Positive word of mouth goes a long way.

For retailers such as Joan Lavers in Toronto or Art Smolensky in Vancouver the task of attracting accounts was achieved through the process of gradually becoming known. Both Art and Joan began modestly, making full use of their immediate friends and their involvement in the immediate community. Art, a former graduate student at the University of British Columbia, lived in the area surrounding the campus while he attended school. He knew and was known by many people. Throughout his student years Art's major preoccupation, other than his studies in chemistry, was photography. Perceiving the market for chemists to be flat, he decided along with his wife and partner to open a camera shop in Kitsilano, British Columbia, in 1970. It took off almost immediately. The university community warmly supported The Lens 'n' Shutter and were particularly impressed by Art's knowledge of photography. As an amateur photographer, he used his personal experience to assist his friends and customers. Customer satisfaction led to word-of-mouth praise for the high quality of service, and ultimately to increased business.

Joan Lavers lived in the Cabbagetown area of Toronto from the early 1970s, and when she decided to go solo, she chose to locate in her neighbourhood. Her children were old enough to be in school, but she still wanted to be close to them. An active, vigorous lady, Joan was active in the community. For several months prior to the opening of her store, she spent a great deal of time talking to the other shopkeepers in the area in order to discover everything possible about their experience. At the same time, having decided to open a kitchen-wares store, Joan visited all future competitors in other parts of the city. She studied their stock, prices, methods of display and general ambiance. By the time she opened in the spring of 1978, the groundwork was complete. There was hardly a soul in Cabbagetown who did not know about her opening. Her husband invited many of his co-workers and associates on Bay Street to the store's first night, and only an hour after opening, fifty people were in the store buying. Word of mouth about the store began to spread.

Art and Joan were selling their store and the products it contained to future customers. All soloists must sell. When you tell someone about your business and when you send away a happy satisfied client, you are selling in the broadest sense of the word.

For those who offer services, selling is equally essential, although the execution is different. For this kind of soloist, the act of selling begins with phone calls. When William Sutton started going solo, he claims he made "a million phone calls" the first week. Sutton was fortunate in that he had no fear of the telephone. Some soloists, especially new ones, have been known to do a little dance around the black demon, shuffling a little to the right, then slipping two quick steps to the left while building up their courage to dial a number. Should this happen to you, this is the time to say, "I'm going to walk through the fear of the unknown and make it to the other side."

Fear stems from the fact that you are often "calling cold." You call cold when you call an absolute stranger and begin to sell yourself or your service. It is important to overcome the fear of "calling cold." You have to make appointments and meet people with whom you will be involved. You have to meet them face to face, shake hands and share conversation with them. They may be suppliers, or they may be future customers.

Eunice Webster of Apex Associates generally makes thirty phone calls a day in order to find customers for her success seminars. Occasionally, she will phone for appointments when seeing a corporation. Eunice forces herself to perform the job of selling herself by planning carefully. In the evening, she compiles a list of the calls to be made the following day. She writes down the individual's name, his company and any additional points that will enable her to be successful in her calls. Eunice covers a lot of territory in a day's work of generating sales because she does her groundwork.

Selling makes it all happen because it generates orders, and orders obtained and fulfilled create accounts. Each account successfully serviced becomes its own centre of profit and a building block of your enterprise. Calling people cold sets the account-building phase of your business in operation.

The kinds of people you need to contact depends on the type of business you have. You have to be creative about finding markets, and for the soloist offering a service, this is a particular challenge. A caterer might want to contact working women who would be potential customers. The question is, where are working women located in large numbers? One might begin by contacting professional women's groups or by seeking write-ups in the publications of corporations (many large firms have in-house publications, these are called "house organs") that employ large numbers of women. A free-lance secretary will want executives to know about the service, a woman offering homemaking services or a firm offering a service related to the home in any way will want to contact homemakers. A public relations person will have to seek out those who require exposure.

If you are operating a retail store, you will, by the same token, need to contact future customers. Where you begin depends on the product. If you are selling something related to business, you need to contact business people.

You may begin to make your initial contacts by using the Yellow Pages, or you may be able to obtain business or industrial directories related to your specific market. Many directories list the names of the president of a given organization, the vice-presidents and their areas of responsibility, marketing and sales managers and other appropriate individuals. One excellent source of information is the annual *Canadian Almanac and Directory* which contains the names, addresses and telephone numbers of virtually every organization in Canada. If you use the Yellow Pages, the receptionists or the company operator will generally give you the names of the people you need to see.

Whenever you are selling, always think of the hard-working persevering salespersons you have known in the past. Remember the door-to-door type knocking on your door with a vacuum cleaner or a set of encyclopedias? The door-to-door salesperson knows that the more doors he or she knocks on, the more people he or she meets, the greater the likelihood of making a sale. When you sell, you may have to use a different technique than the door-to-door salesperson, but your perseverence must be as great. Generally, you will be making presentations to other business people like yourself.

Overcoming shyness is important in selling. Before you became a soloist, you could blend into the woodwork in your office. But not anymore. Successful selling requires using every facet of your personality. A good salesperson will develop the art of talking to just about anyone, and selling gives you the perfect opportunity to make use of skills you never believed you possessed. Remember Aunt Sadie and Uncle Ralph? The only time you saw them was at the annual family reunion. You always felt you had to talk with them if only for a short time. You found you could communicate with them without looking bored. It's a skill that lies buried in almost everyone. Put it to use.

Personal selling is not uncomfortable once you master it. In fact, it can be enjoyable, especially when a potential buyer finally says "yes." Marlys Carruthers, Joyce Krusky and Lynn McLaughlin discovered that buyers were an easy, friendly group, and they enjoyed their sales calls and the learning experience their personal meetings afforded them. In addition to obtaining orders for their book, they made friends along the way.

Sandy Simpson spent long, hard hours in her first years calling newspapers and magazines to get art critics into her gallery. Sandy feels as if she has sent more letters out in one year than the Pentagon (excluding draft notices). Her perseverence paid off. After a year Sandy's new gallery was noticed. Many art critics have praised the innovative nature of Sandy's gallery and can't wait to see what she'll do next.

Your first weeks of selling will be the most difficult, but they will also be the most rewarding. You will come to understand your particular selling style and begin to understand what works for you and what doesn't work for you. There are soloists, such as Len Kubas, who dislike selling at lunch, and others who find that the business lunch is the most effective sales meeting of all.

Selling is the art of establishing working relationships with others. If you are dealing with a wide-open market, the number of working relationships you can establish is only limited by your ability to fulfill the orders and that to a large extent depends on your own energy level and on your firm's ability to expand. For Nathan Zavier and Lynn Hubacheck of Go Fer Enterprises the world is literally their oyster. If they had the energy to utilize all the opportunities that exist for them, they would have to work a twenty-eight-hour day. As it is, they have stringers that they call in when they, themselves, are overbooked.

Cathy Deuber of Home Minders also has a wealth of money-making opportunities. She has developed a lengthy client list in the Eglinton-Yonge area of Toronto and has stringers working for her in other areas of the city. She might be rich, but there are only so many hours in the day, and Cathy hires work out in order to protect her leisure time.

The Sales Trip

Set up your first sales trip by making phone appointments. Don't be shy. Get your list of calls together with your appointment book. Don't book your visits too close together. Next, be certain your presentation is in order, and you feel comfortable with it. If you are as enthusiastic as most soloists, your enthusiasm will fire the person with whom you are meeting. Have a plan, and follow it. Don't allow yourself to say, "I'll make appointments when I get there," or "I'll call from the pay phone across the street." Admit your nervousness and anxiety to yourself. You will overcome them by being prepared. You will make the appointment with John Doe, and you will be punctual. You will know what you are going to say, and you will have a short list of vital points to be covered.

Be yourself to find your own selling style. This is essential. Everyone has a different personality, and everyone sells differently. Books will suggest selling styles, but it is more valuable to discover your own and to develop it fully. What works for you may not necessarily work for another soloist. Be honest about yourself. Do not make appointments for a time of day that does not suit you. Many people are "morning people" and just as many others are "night people." Select your topics for conversation the same way. If you want to get right down to business, do so; if you enjoy drawing people out by discussing sports, politics or other subjects, do so.

Plan your initial trips with plenty of time to spare between appointments. You must make flexible plans. Some calls may take ten minutes, others may take hours. If you suddenly find you are being introduced to the president, the marketing people and the sales force, you can't just leave what might turn out to be a highly successful meeting because you planned two meetings too close together.

Don't be intimidated. Sometimes you'll discover that the person you called arranged for you to meet with someone else. Do not be intimidated by the manner in which people are dressed, the size of their office or their office decor. This is a test of your personality and self-confidence. One president of a large firm had his desk placed on a raised dais so that everyone who came into his office had to look up at him. A person who has to have a higher desk or a higher chair needs adoration. That's his problem, not yours.

Present your product or service clearly. Be polite and confident, state a few words about how your product or services could benefit the individual or company to whom you are making the presentation. Then close your mouth. If you are offering a good product or a needed service, it will sell itself. Answer questions to the best of your ability; questions are an indication that your product or ideas are being considered.

You will need a sense of humour as well. Strange occurrences abound. You may encounter people who are less than sober, who are distracted, who will tell you about their ninety-seven diseases, about their mother-in-law, who will show you pictures of their children or who will make confessions about their job insecurity.

Non-Verbal Communication

The gentleman who must be sitting higher than others delivers a message without actually speaking. He tells those whom he entertains that he wants respect and adoration—he wants everyone to look up to him. He has arranged his room in such a way as to make this happen if not mentally then physically.

Non-verbal communication is important in all societies, but it varies from cultural group to cultural group. In North America three non-verbal indicators are eye contact, distance and time.

Eye contact is extremely important in North American business negotiations. "Look me in the eye if you're telling the truth" is a widely used expression that conveys a North American non-verbal concept. Maintain eye contact. Should you be dealing with those from other cultures, you should be aware that they do not feel the same about eye contact as North Americans. Many cultural groups from the West Indies, the Caribbean or the Indian sub-continent regard eye contact as rude. Arabs traditionally believe that the eyes are the mirror to a man's inner thoughts and, subsequently, tend to carry out business negotiations wearing sun glasses.

North Americans tend to keep a distance of about four feet between one another. An invasion of space can make other people uncomfortable. Many from Latin countries, however, prefer to be closer in terms of space. They tend to lean over, and they want to converse face to face and nose to nose.

Time in North America is an indicator of status. If you are kept waiting over twenty minutes, it indicates you are not thought to be important. On the other hand, ten minutes is the usual waiting period that tells you the person you are waiting to see is important. But if an Italian keeps you waiting for an hour, it means nothing.

In terms of your own presentation, your non-verbal behaviour is extremely important. Lean forward when making a point, keep eye contact, be on time, don't talk with your hand over your mouth and don't fidget with things. Non-verbally, men are allowed to sprawl; women are not. Women ought to sit upright, lean slightly forward and remember to keep their legs together. An impression is created by your totality, and how you handle your body can be as important as what you are saying.

The Do's and Don'ts of "Cold Calling" on the Phone

- Force yourself to call new people and make appointments.
- Be polite. Know what you want to talk about.
- Have a list of the important points in front of you.

- Laugh a little with the person you call. Loosen up; nine times out of ten you're calling a pleasant individual.
- Make a list each night of the people you need to call the next day. Aim to get to see people in person and to set up a number of appointments. Even if you only get three appointments in person per week, it's better than none.
- Give yourself the benefit of the doubt, and assume that all your calls went well.
- Give yourself a reward for making your calls.
- Laugh at your mistakes. The person who can laugh at himself or herself is ten times better off than the person who can't. Even if you stuttered and stammered.

- Don't procrastinate, make the calls and get them over with.
- Don't be arrogant or a know–it–all.
- Don't be overly shy. Summon your personality and be open and frank.
- Don't sit and think how awful you sounded on the phone. There's no time for neurosis. If you made a call that didn't go well, make another and try to improve.
- Don't think you are going through a unique experience. Regardless of how you view yourself, think about the large numbers of people who are worse off.
- Don't be overly serious. Nothing is so serious that you have to be humourless and dour. To summon your humour, envisage the person on the other end of the phone doing something absurd.

The Do's and Don'ts of Personal Selling

- Feel free to learn as you go.
- Do your homework, know your product or service and present it in the best possible light.
- Be yourself, your own personal style is the best style.
- Dress appropriately for the type of people you expect to meet.
- Make sales your number-one priority.
- Follow up on all sales calls.
- Read books on sales techniques.
- Use every ounce of perseverance you possess.

- Don't procrastinate
- Don't be overly critical of yourself.
- Don't be overly serious, things go better with a sense of humour.
- Don't take the nay sayers too much to heart. It's their loss; you know what you're doing.
- Don't be discouraged when you get a "no." Say, "Feel free to contact me if you change your mind?" Or, "Should I call you in several months?"
- Don't pretend you know it all. Listen and learn.
- Don't ram your sales pitch down someone's throat. Be firm, be businesslike, be confident.

Your Track Record

Your company's most valuable asset is the track record you establish. Consider your reputation to be money in the bank and promise yourself that you will never compromise on the quality of your product or service.

Cathy Deuber of Home Minders has twelve stringers in the field working for her. Each is bonded and insured. Cathy makes it a point to call up each customer when the job is complete to find out if everything was done to the satisfaction of the customer. Cathy invites complaints. You cannot correct yourself nor your employees without information. Cathy knows this, and she knows that bad word of mouth can destroy her reputation.

Nancy Thomson feels the same way. Nancy has had to fire two teachers because the quality of their courses fell below Nancy's standards. Her customers pay for a quality course, and without standards, Nancy would lose her company. Even though she hates to fire people, the on-going reputation of her firm is essential.

Sam Blyth has built an imposing record of innovative and exciting tours. Half the year is spent travelling, investigating new locations for his clientele to tour. His care and attention reap dividends when his clients return over and over. He works as hard today as when he first started, but he does not have to establish his credentials any longer. His clients will take Sam at his word, they know they will have a splendid tour.

Building a track record takes time and constant attention to detail. You must be careful not to overextend yourself because if you do, the quality of your work may suffer. It is better to do three assignments well than six badly. If you are producing a product, it is better to sell a quality product and meet your orders than to always be running four weeks behind.

Each assignment for your service or consignment of orders for your business is an investment in the future of your firm. Customers are sacred; the sales they bring you and the money they pay is worth your concentrated efforts now and in the future.

A commitment to your work combined with quality service can eliminate future money problems. Doug Dunbar has no financial worries today because he has always lived up to his commitment to his accounts. His staff is always prepared to work around the clock to fulfill Doug's commitment to overnight service.

> I've always been strong on commitments. Once I make a commitment I will follow it through. If someone has come to me with work, they are depending on me to do it. Come hell or high water, my commitment is to get the job done. I'm sure this has a lot to do with the success of the business.

Calculate for yourself what you can be worth in dollars by always concentrating on doing your assignments well, or delivering your product on time.

When sales of Gary Dahl's Pet Rocks started to climb, he and his family spent days and nights filling orders as rapidly as possible. They could have approached the task in a leisurely, non-hurried manner, but being a week late on a delivery would constitute a loss of revenue for everyone concerned. Millions of Pet Rocks were sold because Dahl concentrated on fast, efficient service to his customers.

As time goes by, your clientele will grow. When Audrey Grant started The Toronto Bridge Club she took her time too. But those who did come in the beginning had a good time and were pleased with her service. Now her tables are full. Audrey did not ask for overnight success, she built her business steadily. Three new people a night was fine. If they had a good time, they would tell their friends, and Audrey would shortly double the amount of new faces in a few short weeks. For Audrey, building a business is concentrating on the task at hand.

> Sometimes you think, well, I just can't do this. But running a business is like learning to play the piano. You just don't think about what you can't do. The more you train yourself to forget the mass of worries you have and concentrate on the task at hand, the better sense you get of the business. When you concentrate, the business seems to take care of itself. You do the job at hand and complete it, then you're free to go on to the next job.

Using Your Contacts

A number of soloists find they can take lucrative accounts with them when they leave a job to go solo, though such individuals should check with their lawyers about the exact moral and legal implications. It is grand to be respected by people you have worked with for years, respected enough for them to follow you wherever you go.

Walter Schroeder's company Dominion Bond Rating Service Ltd. evolved out of his seven years with Wood Gundy. His job there was to analyze and investigate Canadian companies in order that Gundy clients could be advised whether or not to invest.

> By the time I left Wood Gundy I had visited every major corporation in Canada. I had also met with many of the portfolio investment people and the people who run the pension funds.
>
> Once we got started, I called up all the contacts I had made, described the service I was creating, and asked them to subscribe. We had already done ratings on one hundred of the largest companies. We explained how it worked and what the ratings meant. Because of my reputation at Gundy, they were willing to subscribe to the service.
>
> We picked up around half the accounts we hoped to get. It took us another six months to build up our base, and thus be able to turn a profit.

William Sutton had a similar experience when he started his own insurance agency.

> When I knew I was starting my own business, I received sound

legal advice on the problem of getting clients from my last job. I knew that many of my accounts would be upset at my leaving, and I was sure they would want to follow me. I could not solicit their business while I was still at my previous job; they would get you for that–making use of internal information. The day I left the company, however, all the information, names and phone numbers, was in my mind, and that's perfectly legal.

A friend warned me at the time to be prepared for disappointments. He suggested that I must have some guys on my mental list for whom there was no question whatsoever about them joining me. It's true that perhaps clients even tell you, at some point, they will come with you when you're on your own. They won't. They will all offer good reasons why they can't switch agencies at this time. My friend was right. At the same time, accounts I never would have thought would come to me did.

There was one account especially that I "knew" I would get on day one. If all else failed, there was a piece of business from the National Hockey League that I knew was mine. That one certain account took me over three years to land, but I finally got it.

Use contacts from previous jobs to develop an account base, even if your new business is in a different field. After all, people that you have worked with in previous business relationships know the kind of work you are capable of and may well become accounts when you are in business for yourself.

Secretaries and administrative assistants especially have ample opportunities to develop contacts while working for others. Think about such contacts and ask yourself if they would make likely accounts for you. You can take advantage of past contacts just as you take advantage of past experience.

You may not even have to hustle to sign up old contacts. Joanna Campion needed an advertising agency intimately familiar with direct mail. She found one that was perfect for her needs, and they assigned two bright young executives to her company. When these two people left the agency to start their own, Joanna quickly moved her account. They did not solicit her business while they were still employed by others, but Joanna knew them and wanted to retain the same quality of service they had been rendering. They didn't have to ask her. She cared about the success of her business and enjoyed working with them.

Use your contacts. But do be careful not to step beyond the bounds of honourable business practice. Do not solicit accounts while you are still employed by others. Do not try to take accounts away from a former boss if you are selling exactly the same product or offering exactly the same service. If, of course, the client wishes to follow you, it is quite ethical to accept the business.

Chapter 12

Getting the Word Out

Technically speaking, advertising is paid for, and publicity is free. But both call attention to you and your business. Neither advertising nor publicity is as difficult as many soloists imagine.

Advertising

Print: Such advertising includes newspapers, magazines, flyers and brochures. The cost of it varies greatly, and you should remember that the cost of advertising becomes one of the overheads of the business. Thus, costing out the ad and attempting to assess its value is important in order to maintain a cost-efficient business.

Apart from cost, the single, most important factor in print advertising is the advertising vehicle itself. A bookseller would not place an ad in a magazine that dealt with motorcycles (unless the books were directly related to motorcycles). Nor does one advertise jockstraps in women's magazines. Publications have specific markets, and advertising ought to be geared to the same markets. *Choose an advertising vehicle that suits your business.*

Your ad should be clear, concise and contain the following:

- Who you are (the name of the business);
- Where you are (the address);
- When you are open (the hours);
- What you are selling;
- How to purchase your product or service (phone number, charge cards); and
- Any other pertinent information, i.e., a special sale.

Newspapers and magazines charge by the column-inch for block advertising. Rates can be obtained from the specific publication or from *Canadian Advertising Rates and Data*, a Maclean-Hunter

Publication which covers all print media in Canada as well as radio and television stations. CARD, as it is known in the industry, is laid out in subject areas and can, therefore, be useful in finding the right advertising vehicle. It is an expensive publication, but you may be able to get an old copy and make good use of it. The rates will have changed, of course, but the subject areas will not, and even the old rates will give you an idea of costs.

If the advertising vehicle prepares the ad for you, it will probably cost more than if you can provide the newspaper or magazine with "camera-ready copy." Camera-ready copy is exactly what the term implies—an ad completely ready for reproduction. Many firms, large and small, specialize in producing ad layouts. These should be investigated, and the costs should be compared.

It is much less expensive to advertise in the classified sections of newspapers and magazines. Many newspapers and magazines have, in addition to their general classified sections, specialized areas such as *The Globe and Mail's* "Business to Business" or the "Help for Homeowners" columns in a variety of papers.

Flyers are especially useful. They can be typed on a typewriter or typeset. Once you have your mock-up, it can be mimeographed, printed on an offset press or photostated. The same methods can be used in the production of brochures. There are many free-lance graphic arts people who do this kind of work.

A point to consider is the cost of delivering flyers or brochures. Again, there are firms that specialize in their distribution.

Direct mail is one method of delivery. You establish a mailing list or purchase one, and the flyers or brochures are mailed directly to the prospective client. But remember, your piece of mail competes with every other piece of mail. To be successful, the prospective client must read it.

When planning any advertising campaign, these steps should always be followed:

1. Ascertain who you want to reach.
2. Make a list of the newspapers, magazines, in-house publications or special publications that will reach your market.
3. Call each publication and investigate a) the cost of block advertising if they prepare the ad; b) the cost of block

advertising if you submit camera-ready copy; c) the cost of classified advertising; d) the circulation of the advertising vehicle. (Do not take their word for circulation figures unless the vehicle is a small local publication. Circulation figures are verified by various agencies, so ask if they have verified circulation.)

4. Decide on a vehicle and price the cost of one ad, a series of repeat ads or discounts given to regular advertisers.
5. Prepare the ad, or have it prepared by a graphics person. Be aware that if the ad is in colour, there will be added costs. (Black on white is the most reasonable. Two-colour and three-colour are also available, and full colour is the most expensive.)
6. Place the advertising.
7. Monitor the response.

With flyers and brochures there are added costs and considerations. If the flyer or brochure is being printed, you should investigate what is known as the "print break." You may decide on 5,000 brochures because you think that number will be less costly then the 10,000 you actually need. But the cost of the extra 5,000 may be much less than you imagine, since on the second 5,000 you are not paying for the brochure to be "set." You are paying only for labour and for paper. Once the press is running, the cost of the extra 5,000 is negligible. Most printers have minimum print runs, and the cost per 1,000 decreases considerably with quantity. It could, for example, cost $500 for 5,000 brochures and only $650 for 10,000. The print break is the number at which the cost per 100 or the cost per 1,000 becomes cheaper.

How do you assess the effectiveness of an ad? Many retail operations ask the reader to bring the ad to the store—"Bring this ad for a 10 per cent discount on your new chrome-plated widget!" Or, you may choose to ask your clients directly where they heard of you. Some businesses utilize short questionnaires: "Did you hear about us by word of mouth? Through advertising? Or were you just passing by?"

You cannot assess the cost effectiveness of advertising over the short term. You have to place your ads, distribute your flyers or brochures and compile your assessment over at least a three-month period.

How much advertising you need depends on the type of operation you have. For many, a repeat ad in a local paper or magazine is sufficient. For others, advertising is unnecessary altogether.

Cathy Deuber of Home Minders advertises regularly in the classified section of *Toronto Life* and has tried other vehicles as well, but she finds the regular *Toronto Life* ad to be sufficient to back up her publicity and word-of-mouth recommendations.

Joan Lavers of What's Cooking? sends out flyers and maintains a mailing list of all the customers who have shopped at her store. Since she runs a local store, her advertising efforts are concentrated on developing as many customers as possible in her own community. She has also tried advertising in the television section of *The Globe and Mail*, along with other retail shops in her area. Such joint advertising has been successful, and she and the other business people can share costs and develop the idea of shopping in their specific vicinity.

Radio: The cost of all advertising is based on the number of people the ad will reach, so the cost of radio advertising depends on the station and the size of its audience.

If the announcer at the station reads your ad, it will probably be less costly than if you have a tape prepared. What you say in your ad is generally what you would say in print advertising (who, what, when, where and how), but you might want special effects—music, rockets—that add to the expense.

Spot announcements, generally for saturation advertising, are the least expensive, but these can't convey much hard information. But if you run a record store, you might choose spot advertising on a popular station so that the announcer would break in now and again with, "Buy these and other records at Jack's!" The audience will soon come to associate Jack's with records.

Radio stations give discounts for the number of times the ads are read in any given twenty-four-hour period. As in printing, the ads often become less expensive with quantity. Also like print advertising, radio has distinct markets. Rock stations reach an audience between the ages of twelve and eighteen, more sedate stations that play nostalgic music reach an older market. Find out who listens to what before you place your advertising.

Television: These types of ads are the most expensive; so expensive that many people have returned to the print medium. The first cost is the production cost. The least you can get away with is a spot, still ad—a photograph of the product with a voiceover. You know the type—there is a set of knives, for example, and the voiceover informs the viewer of the merits of the product, the telephone number which can be called to place an order or the post office box the viewer can write to, along with the price and usually a bonus. K-Tel is famous for this type of advertising, though in a more elaborate style. It is no more and no less than televised direct-mail selling.

The next most reasonable form of television advertising is the do-it-yourself ad on a local station. This is the type of ad made famous by used-car salesmen. Undoubtedly, television advertising by local business on local channels is effective.

The production costs of the above are not great, but the production costs of other forms of television advertising are extremely expensive. Animation, for example, costs about $10,000 a second, and that's before you pay for the ad to be aired. It is impossible to give an indication of production costs because they vary and are changing constantly.

An ad purchased on network television is the most expensive. But there are all kinds of variations here as well. The cost depends on the length of the ad, on the number of network stations on which it will appear, on the time of day (prime-time hours are the most expensive) and on the program. An ad appearing on the Johnny Carson show (even if shown locally) will cost more because the viewing audience is known to be large. In Canada, a thirty-second network ad (one that appears on all stations) during a popular prime-time show runs into thousands of dollars. In the United States, it can run to almost half a million.

Plan your advertising campaign carefully. Design it for your specific business and assess your ads during a three-month period. You cannot judge an advertising vehicle strictly by its appearance or cost. Joan Lavers, for example, advertised regularly in an inexpensive publication and soon realized she was throwing her money away. One month she put a 30 per cent discount coupon in her ad. No one returned with the coupon, and she realized her ad wasn't pulling in customers.

Webster defines advertising as "a means of calling public attention in order to arouse a desire to purchase." Regardless of the type of business you have, or the amount of money you have budgeted for advertising, you must perform this task efficiently.

Publicity

Publicity generates "word of mouth." When people speak highly of your service or product, you have already begun a publicity campaign.

You must ask yourself, "Am I news? Is there a story in what I'm doing?" Lynn Hubacheck and Nathan Zavier of Go Fer Enterprises established a large number of accounts as a result of newspaper stories about them.

Newspapers and magazines cover what's happening in the community and can give you free media exposure with stories that relate to your business. Basically, such stories fall into that area of journalism known as "human interest," though some may appear in the business or family section. Do not be discouraged if you feel you are doing something "ordinary." As is often said in public relations, "there is always a handle"—some angle or hook your story can be hung on.

To find a handle, the following questions should be asked:

1. Is there something unique about yourself? Did you once work for a big firm? Are you a veteran? Are you a single parent supporting children? Are you making money from a former hobby?
2. Is there something unique about your business or product?
3. Is there something unique about your clientele?
4. Are you creating jobs in your community?

If the answers to these questions indicate that there is a story in what you are doing, let people in the media know about it by sending out a press release.

Your press release should be sent to newspapers, magazines,

radio and television stations. Address it to *The Editor*, in the case of print publications, or phone and get specific names for the reporter who covers stories of local human interest, the business editor, the editor of the family section, etc. For radio and television, send it to *The News Editor*, or again phone for specific names.

Your press release should be no longer than one page. Its opening paragraph should say who you are and what you are doing. Its second paragraph should elaborate on who you are, and the third should detail whatever unique or newsworthy aspect of your business you have determined from asking yourself the above questions. You will have a last line (indented) that reads, "For further information, call: (your name and phone number)."

Send your press releases to *appropriate* media. If you are starting a small local business utilize weekly newspapers and local magazines as well as local radio and television stations. Be realistic. If you are opening a hot dog restaurant close to a factory or school, you will want a story that will reach the workers or the students. Do not expect to be on national television because you offer homemade chili sauce in your restaurant.

Nancy Thomson sent out a press release, and it caught an assignment editor's fancy.

> When the story appeared on my course, it listed the phone number of the Investment Dealers Association (where my classes would be held). The article appeared on a Saturday, and on Monday the switchboard was jammed. Andy Kneiwasser, the president of IDA, grabbed me and started jumping up and down, saying, "You've done it! You've done it! Women are terrific!" Over eight hundred phone calls were received because of that article.
>
> We took the names and addresses of all the callers, printed up a brochure and sent it to them. I was prepared to teach three classes of twenty-five people each. We received two hundred and eighty-four cheques in the mail, and it almost broke my heart to send back over two hundred of them. Each returned cheque was accompanied by a letter offering more courses in a few months' time. Virtually everyone returned their cheque and registered for the course three months later.

Despite the doom and gloom that appears daily, the press is open and eager to publish upbeat human-interest stories. A new company can be news, and success sells.

Of course, not all newspaper stories are as effective as the one that appeared about Nancy Thomson. Brian Brittain owns Tranquility Tanks in Toronto. A tranquility tank is a tank in which the customer lies suspended in liquid, in silence and in the dark. The client achieves total relaxation. It is a treatment for stress. Brian has used several forms of advertising but found hand circulars to be the most effective for him.

> When I started, a few reporters came from *The Globe and Mail.* They went into the tank, loved it, and wrote it up in the paper. After their story appeared, several other newspapers sent reporters and feature writers. Their stories appeared, and we were quite happy. But we didn't get any additional business.
>
> Around the same time, the movie "Altered States" was playing. My partner and I would go to the theatre every night while the crowds were waiting in line to get in. We'd walk up and down the line, handing out our flyers. We attracted a number of customers.
>
> After two years in business, we have a good idea who our clients are. A number are university students. When we print up a set of flyers, we plaster them around the campus. We also advertise in campus newspapers.

When Doug Dunbar opened College Copy Shop in 1968, he used flyers to generate his first business.

> My brother and I had been working all weekend putting up flyers around the university. We put them up everywhere we could—on billboards, under car-wipers, in the residences, on telephone poles, everywhere. We were getting responses even as we put them up. By Saturday afternoon we already had work in the shop and we weren't officially open until Monday. We still didn't have all our equipment.
>
> On Monday morning there was more work to be done. Later that morning the equipment finally arrived and was installed by mid-afternoon.
>
> Since those early days, we have gained from word of mouth. People that were in the university are now in business.

> They left school, and remembered the quality of service they received from College Copy, and they came back. We have never actively sought to expand our business, but as our original customer base grew and moved up, they took us with them.
>
> We advertise in the Yellow Pages. At first it was a small ad, but it is a bit larger now. We advertise in campus newspapers. Once when the company was young we took out an ad in *The Globe and Mail.* It resulted in some business in the mail from Manitoba. We were all surprised, but we did the job. We now occasionally get jobs from the Maritimes, the Territories and out West.

Finding the correct advertising scheme for your business is a matter of finding what works specifically for you. For Doug Dunbar it was flyers, then word of mouth, occasional ads and a constant ad in the Yellow Pages. Sam Blyth, tour operator, uses word of mouth plus the occasional ad in *The Globe and Mail.*

> I don't compete against the travel agencies. For example, I'll never book a one- or two-week package holiday to the Caribbean. That's not my business. But if you want to climb mountains in Nepal or have a personally conducted bicycle tour of China, I can help you.
>
> Virtually all of my tour business comes through word of mouth. If you can provide two or three unusual and exciting weeks for a customer, you can be certain they will talk about it for years to come. Eventually a friend will want an unusual and exciting holiday, and they will give me a call.
>
> For the other parts of my business, whether it's the Show Train or being entertained as you travel down the Mississippi River on the *Mississippi Belle*, I advertise heavily in *The Globe and Mail* which is a national newspaper. Still most of my business is either repeat or word of mouth. People enjoy telling their friends when they've had a good time.

Word of mouth is the most effective form of advertising, and the only form that cannot be purchased. It must be developed on a day-to-day, customer-to-customer basis. When you initiate your business, you gain customers through paid advertising, and these customers or clients form your account base. But each client must be satisfied. They must pass the word about you, and they must return themselves.

Brad, Laurie and Gail Greenwood of Greenwood's Books in Edmonton have spent the last three years painstakingly building their clientele. They have worked hard at understanding their clients' needs, and they have developed a loyal clientele that returns to buy books. The Greenwoods spend hours poring over book catalogues in an attempt to match their selections to their customers' interests. Their goal is a full-service bookstore where their customers can always find the books they want.

Joan Lavers of What's Cooking? built a loyal following of customers through service, dependability, quality products and information. Joan's customers depend on her cooking expertise. She continues to advertise her products and services, but her loyal customers are the foundation of her business.

Advertising is more than merely putting an ad in the paper and hoping for the best. It is following through on the ad by providing the kind of service you advertise.

Networking

Networking is a term used to describe mutually advantageous relationships in business. The co-operative spirit is alive and well among soloists. Soloists can share customers and co-operate on advertising costs, rents and equipment. When two soloists share client lists, leads, ideas, support and good old-fashioned labour, they both benefit. Sometimes after years of competitive employment in a large corporation, soloists find a renewed sense of sharing through the small business network.

George Prokos of the Public Relations Board of Canada is an active "networker."

> It's nice having relationships with people in business which are mutually helpful. I have such a relationship with Richard Skinulus with whom I share office space. If I were on my own, it would cost more. I would rather share office space because I like people, and I don't like working alone. There are times when I have to be quiet, when I have to write, but that isn't always the case. I am so much more of a business person if I

have relationships with other people that are understanding and enabling.

I know Richard can do certain things and I suggest to him, "Why don't you see so and so," and he comes back to me another day and says, "Why don't you lunch with so and so," and I go out and see his contact. We all benefit that way, it's all part of networking.

Michael Gowling has been networking all his life. He recounts networking experiences in Bogotá, Columbia, and Canada:

I was constantly under the nose of everyone at the American Embassy in Bogotá and much of it was social. My work came through volunteer work with the Community Players of Bogotá. I got to meet all the advertising directors of multinational firms who advertised in the program. Since I had done advertising back in Hamilton, I was able to offer them a service. Because I could speak English and I was competent, I got a lot of work out of them. I got work purely on my sociability and my ability to work a cocktail party. I also got work by playing bridge, and I still do that to this day.

I continue to see clients on a social basis; we have respect for each other personally and we're all upwardly mobile. I make no bones about it, I ask those in my network to speak in my lecture series, because their names add weight to the series. It's good for me to have big names, and it is a career move for them. It's insurance for them. They are going to get recognition and their companies are going to have to deal with that when it comes time for their raise. How can they say no? They know we're all going places together.

When I worked for Northern Telecom for the first time, I did a program with the sales engineer for Western Canada. We did all these live demonstrations and put him on tape. We made him look good. Now he's risen to the position where he has the buying power to buy my product. I can be sure he's not going to go out and hire someone else. It's now a risk for him *not* to deal with me. I'm a known quantity. He knows I make him look good. That's what business is all about.

There's that social savvy that's necessary, as well as honesty and sincerity. It's more than just dealing with price. It's an honesty of dealing with personality. People know I'm not a person who's out to screw them or add twenty per cent to the budget. They know I'm making us all look good. That works well for anyone in a consulting capacity.

When I do a good job, I ask people for letters of recommendations too. I do a lot of freebee stuff solely on that as well. I will be glad to speak at your seminar and tell your audience what they need and want to know. After that, just write me a letter of recommendation that I can use to promote myself. I gotta promote myself.

For some soloists, a previous network does not exist. The opportunities to hook into an existing network, however, are vast. It can be a local business association, the Chamber of Commerce, a professional association or even a bridge club or sports club. Any and all of these organizations can provide the soloist with an ever widening range of contacts. It can also provide good friends, as Joan Lavers discovered.

Before I opened my store, I joined the Ward Seven Business Association. I only spend a few hours a month with them, but the rewards have been great. First of all, the problems of the community, if there are any, can hurt me. We'll meet once a month and discuss the business atmosphere in the area and what we can do to make it better. Afterwards, we usually go to one of the pubs in the neighbourhood and share our experiences. We all support each other's business in that way.

To attract new business to the area, we have organized, once a year, the "Cabbagetown Cultural Festival." A publicity committee sends out press releases to all the papers and radio and television. All the merchants have special sales for that weekend, and there are also marching bands, clowns and games for all visitors. One year a couple from Pontiac, Michigan, came to my store because of a write-up in a local paper about the Cultural Festival. They saw the description of my store, liked it and made a good purchase before they left.

Michael Woods has built his successful accounting practice, in part, by joining and networking. His business was assisted in the beginning by friends who needed his services, then he began joining and meeting prospective accounts.

Squash clubs can provide some excellent accounts. I'll join a squash club or a tennis club, not specifically to hunt for business, but because I need the relaxation. But I do get to meet many people. The more people I meet in these situations, the greater the likelihood that they need an accountant or have a friend who needs an accountant.

It's just so important to be known. These contacts and friends that I make may give me some of their accounting business for their own reasons. They may believe they can get it cheaper by using me, or maybe they feel they are doing me a favour, or maybe they like me. They will come to me and say, 'Here you go, do some work.'

If I do a good job, they are going to tell three of their friends. Next year, rather than having one client, I may have three clients. In the third year, I may have nine.

I also display my services in any type of forum I can get. I'll go to companies and give general tax seminars to their sales people around tax time each year. The salesmen love it because they get tax ideas. I love it because at least twenty to thirty of them call me up and ask me to do their tax returns.

For some soloists, such as Kelly LaBrash, being a Canadian becomes part of their networking process.

My belief is that if a Canadian company can hire another Canadian company, they will. There is a strong national feeling in the security business. For example, we handle the uniformed security at the head offices of four banks: the Bank of Montreal, the Bank of Nova Scotia, Canadian Imperial Bank of Commerce and the Royal Bank. We had to bid against American companies for the job, and I know we won the contracts because we are Canadian.

In their defense, the American companies do hire all Canadians, but their profits do go south, or wherever. My profits stay in Canada.

Andy Crosbie and Angus McKay have made excellent use of their Canadian network.

When the C.R.T.C. (Canadian Radio and Telecommunications Commission) enacted Canadian Content rules, it was the best thing that could ever have happened for the recording industry here. It's a great song, but how many times can you listen to *Snow Bird* before you start climbing walls?

> Under the "CanCon" rules, sixty per cent of air time is devoted to Canadian music and/or performers. It doesn't mean that we have a free ride by any radio station. There's some fairly stiff competition for that air time. We still have to get the very best out of an artist and our production standards must be high. If we have a good record, we know that we'll get the exposure, and hopefully sell a few records.

Some entrepreneurs are fortunate in that there is a ready-made network that can be called upon. They have their families behind them, rooting for them and even contributing many hours of work. For Audrey Grant, her family is essential. She couldn't run her business without the help of both her parents and her teen-aged daughters.

> My mother is my accountant, and it's fantastic. It's like sending in the reinforcements. She did things for me that I couldn't have done nor could have afforded to have done for me. But she helps out, and that's great. I think in this economy when things are going under, often it's the family businesses that are the ones that survive. It's the family working together that makes things a go.
>
> My children are very much part of the business. My brother helps, and my husband helps. Everyone's part of a thing that's happening. My family is behind me one hundred per cent. It's just fabulous.
>
> My parents are retired, and they aren't bored. They have too much to do. They go and make the bank deposits, they help me shop and cook, and they take my car in when it needs repairs and help me by going to the cleaners. My dad's in his seventies and my Mom's sixty-two, and they work here three days a week. Some nights it's three generations, grandmother, mother and daughter all working together at the front desk.

When you are an employee, part of your social life revolves around your fellow workers. You are known and respected. Your network of business friends and associates will fill a similar role in your new life as a soloist. Your network will become an "expanded" office, and you will meet and create new working relationships. After all, businesses are created and developed by people working together.

Your accountant, your lawyer, your clients and your suppliers can become your friends.

Tips for Advertising, Publicity and Networking

1. Don't be shy about blowing your own horn. You are the best advertisement for your business. Start spreading the word of mouth yourself.
2. Be on a list. If you have a business phone, you should be listed in the Yellow Pages. Also consider block advertising. If your classification is unique, you may be the only one listed. See to it that you are listed in business directories.
3. Never look a gift horse in the mouth. Always try to be written up in local publications. If you are different enough, you might try national newspapers and magazines as well.
4. Write and distribute press releases.
5. Join organizations that can help provide a useful network. These include business and professional organizations, trade organizations, charitable committees, service clubs and religious groups.
6. Wave your Maple Leaf! Many prefer to buy Canadian.
7. Utilize your family's talents and friends.
8. Plan your advertising carefully together with your publicity program. Allot a certain amount of money for advertising and the printing of flyers and brochures. Remember, money spent on advertising and materials for publicity is tax exempt.
9. Be consistent and advertise regularly. Try to establish a symbol or slogan by which people identify you.
10. Above all, be innovative. "Necessity is the mother of invention."

Chapter 13
Employees

You decided to become your own boss for a good reason. You wanted to realize your own dreams and achieve personal freedom. Beware! *Employees can limit your freedom.* Equally, they can enhance it. It's all up to you. You're the boss.

In the last several decades workers have managed to win substantial wage increases with built-in cost of living increases, health insurance, dental insurance, unemployment benefits, as well as maternity leave. Consequently, employees are far more expensive than in any other period in recent history and not only in terms of money but in terms of paperwork as well. This is not to say that the gains made by labour have not been just and legitimate. Few reasonable people would argue the injustice done the labourer, especially in light of the record of the past. But as a small-business person you are not to blame for other people's past mistakes.

As a soloist seeking help you must be willing to pay an honest wage for an honest job, and you must adhere to government regulations which vary from jurisdiction to jurisdiction. If an employee believes he or she can make more elsewhere, let the employee go. You are not competing with large corporations on either product or wage. But you must be fair.

The object of hiring an employee is to get the job done in a manner that is satisfactory to you. Nothing more, nothing less. Sometimes a soloist will spend more time teaching an employee the business than the employee will spend on the business. This is counter-productive. You must find a person who will do just exactly what you want done.

As a beginning soloist you probably cannot afford to offer a prospective employee an elaborate "package," and you may follow the example of many soloists who prefer to hire occasional help or free lancers for specific jobs.

Soloists are individualistic souls and usually do not want their companies to grow into large corporations. Growing too large presents too many problems.

Mikki West of Pamper Yourself and Dianne Shore of Dianne Shore Interior Planning Ltd. like co-operative employees or no employees at all. Mikki explains it this way:

> I want to work side by side with my fellow man. I don't want to be above anyone, and I don't want to be below anyone. I am just fine working side by side.

Fred Bird has been less than thrilled as a large employer, and now he has drastically limited his staff.

> I have two employees right now, and I like it that way. With the partnership, we were up to seventeen employees. Every Friday, it was scary, especially when we slowed down.
>
> With employees, I finally discovered why people don't talk about their salaries. No sooner would I give someone a raise than others would find out. I would be bombarded by these people saying that they had to talk to me. They wanted more money too.
>
> When the partnership ended, I got rid of most of the staff. With the staff I have now, I pay them a regular paycheque, and they also receive a percentage of what they shoot. They're happy as hell with this arrangement and so am I.

Michael Woods is in a position that as an accountant whether or not he wants employees he has to have them.

> In an accounting business you have to have employees. I've gone through periods when I typed all the financial statements, did all the bookkeeping, completed tax returns, and typed and mailed out the bill. That's a waste of time. I'm caught in a situation because whether I want employees or not, I've got to have them, so I can be free to do what I want to do. When there's no alternative and you must have employees, you must make the best of the situation. I try to do it by having fun.
>
> I try to joke with Shawn during the day, and occasionally I sit down and have a cup of coffee with her. It's great to have someone around when I feel like letting off steam. When a client gets me down, I'll yell and bitch to Shawn about it.
>
> A properly motivated employee makes money for me, so

it's my job to see that the employee is properly motivated. I do that by overextending their skills as much as possible. Make them run as hard as they possibly can to keep up, and keep them interested in what they're doing.

I don't know how easy I am to work for. I'm a fairly moody bastard and those who know me can tell when I don't want to talk to anybody.

Doug Dunbar has over thirty-five employees working for him at his three College Copy locations.

Finding good employees is an extremely difficult problem. The young people whom we mostly employ do not seem to be willing to work hard, or put any quality and effort into their work. I think it's a common complaint among other businesses too.

The best employees I have tend to come from two distinct areas: small towns and foreign countries. The expectations of people brought up in the city are far higher, things are easier for them, and perhaps they are not used to working. I believe that the discipline in small towns and ethnic communities is far more strict than it is in Canadian cities.

I have had to fire people a few times, and I don't like doing it. I resist it as much as possible. I know the right methods of dealing with staff—to help them, encourage them, show them their good points, encourage by example, instead of coming down hard (I'm not very good at that). We have never dismissed anyone for lack of work, only because of on-the-job performance. They have been unable to live up to the standards and quality of service I want my customers to have.

I don't like the word president. I consider myself a co-worker with more responsibilities than the other fellows. They call me "boss," and I don't like it. I guess it's my background, personality and character, but I don't find it demeaning to lug in cartons, personally transfer paper supplies from one store to another, hold the door open for customers. At times maybe I should use a courier service, but by doing it myself, I know it is done right. Even with three shops in Toronto, administrating is not a full-time job. I still serve customers behind the counter, run off copies, fix the machines. It's a way of keeping in touch with the business. It also serves as a model to the staff.

I could hire someone to take care of my administrative

duties, but I doubt I could get someone with the same dedication as an owner. I'm very much service-minded and sitting behind a desk is not performing a service for the customers.

Joan Lavers has her share of difficulties finding the right kind of employees for her kitchen shop.

I have been quite fortunate with the people I've hired, although no one has stayed for more than six months. That's the biggest problem: the constant training and retraining. People don't stay long in a retail store because the wages are low, and you can't afford to have them full-time either.

Because my kitchen store is oriented towards personal service, I can't just have a kid behind the cash. There are thousands of kitchen utensils and my employees have to know how to cook and use them. They have to answer any questions the customers may have. So I look for housewives and older women who have plenty of cooking experience and don't really depend on the salary to live. Still, it takes me two months to fully train someone to the point where I can comfortably leave them in the store alone.

I have to get out to see suppliers and check the competition and just go out for personal reasons, so I really have to have staff. Even with an employee I still have to be in the store quite a bit because personal rapport is the backbone of my business. I think I'm successful because of it. People are downright angry and disappointed with me if I'm not at the store when they come in with a cooking problem that only I can solve.

Brian Brittain is in a double-bind situation. He needs employees who can handle taking care of customers who go into his tranquility tanks, but he doesn't have enough of a cash flow to handle paying high salaries.

I'm boss, which to me means being able to lead. I try to create a context for the staff, which by my example they are able to follow. It serves to motivate them to put out their best. Sometimes it is difficult. We need a reasonably sophisticated individual working here, but we can't pay the going rate. At

> times, these strains are difficult to reconcile. Right now, we can't pay more than $4 per hour, but because of the nature of the work, we just can't get a sixteen-year-old high school student. We are dealing with fairly sensitive issues around here.
>
> I can't afford to give my staff financial strokes, so I try to give them other kinds of strokes. I enjoy catching them doing something right, and telling them. They appreciate the recognition.

William Sutton, according to his staff, is one of the best bosses they ever had. He has a small office, and the daily pressure and deadlines are intense.

> I try to employ people I like, people I enjoy, who I believe can be strong contributors to the business. It gives me great joy to see people progress, learning new talents and being able to advance themselves.
>
> I really dislike having to sit down with an employee and have strong words. I don't think anyone likes telling an employee to shape up or ship out. But, if I must, I just grit my teeth, put it off for a day or two, and do it.
>
> The most difficult part of business for most people is motivating staff, being sensitive to their problems and perceiving their problems. I'm a little insensitive from time to time. My wife will call me and ask what's wrong with so-and-so? She seems a little down today. I'll get out of my office and take a look, and my wife is right. I just haven't noticed it. That part of running a business comes less naturally to me than the technicalities of the business.
>
> I don't work as hard at motivation as I should. I do try to recruit self-motivated, self-starting people. I've been fortunate in that there has been very little turnover since I started. Only one person has left for other than personal reasons, and we both agreed at the time that she wasn't cut out for the job.
>
> My greatest problem is finding more people like me. If I could find three more like me, we would be off to the races.

With a staff exceeding one thousand at certain times, Kelly LaBrash has become the consummate boss. He expresses the problems of bosses everywhere:

It feels good having employees. It is particularly rewarding when you realize many of our people could not get jobs anywhere else. For example, we'll have a man in his later forties. Maybe he's on workman's compensation, and he has a bad arm, maybe he has been injured. He's a good hard-working man, but he can't get a job. If his background is clean, he can get a job with us. Many of our jobs are not that demanding; a number are routine security. All the man has to do is watch, and if someone breaks into the building, he simply calls the police. Other security functions, with computers, for example, require highly trained and highly skilled people.

This has always been a low-paying business. Over the years we have sought higher rates and are now able to pay better money. When we first started, it was a tough business. We were being low-balled all the time by the big American companies.

Fortunately the pendulum has swung. If you continue to pay people a minimum wage, you cannot discipline or direct, but once you start paying, say, double the minimum wage, you attract better people. Most of our people now earn six to seven dollars an hour, and we use a large number of part-time people, school teachers and university students. They are excellent types who are willing to work twenty-four hours on a weekend. They're conscientious, and they need the money. It works out well for everyone.

We've had problems with employees, but nothing serious. I can sometimes have a thousand in the field working at one time. They are in vulnerable spots, and you're bound to have some problems, people being what they are, but the problems are mostly minor.

In the past our greatest problem was recruiting good people to work for us. Now that times are tough, we find that we are attracting better educated and better skilled people. Recruitment is not the problem it used to be.

The one major drawback to having so large a staff is that I have to have two or three people working full-time doing nothing but paperwork, since the government requires so much information, so many forms—social insurance to O.H.I.P. and what have you. Another problem is that with so many people who are hired or not hired in a given year, we occasionally have to justify our hiring practices. Our applicants must be screened carefully, and it's possible there is a blemish on their record. We can't hire them, but suddenly we have the human rights commission on us.

There are a thousand problems out in the field. I find I have to delegate the pressure. If I didn't, I'd go crazy. We're being sued right now by a competitor for taking one of their key people. I simply hire a lawyer and let him deal with it. For the rest, I have a general manager, an assistant G.M., area managers and a group of supervisors who are constantly checking on the performance of the men in the field. They all have fairly wide areas of authority, and are expected to solve problems on the spot. When a problem gets to me, it has got to be pretty bad. Fortunately I don't get many of them.

To hire or not to hire employees depends on the nature of your business and on your own personality. Kelly LaBrash and Doug Dunbar would have no business without employees. Joan Lavers would be locked up in her store and would be unable to visit her competition and keep abreast of her business. Nancy Thomson would be limited to one course every six months without teachers and clerical workers in addition to sales people on her staff.

Other soloists neither need nor want employees. Many dislike the idea of taking full responsibility for another's livelihood.

Again, beware. Do not hire employees unless you have specific work to be done or unless you need to be freed for a certain amount of time. The burdens of being "the Boss" are something to avoid. But if you must get help, follow these general principles.

Tips on Hiring

1. Before you hire anyone, make a list of what you need done and outline in full the responsibilities you want your prospective employee to take. Ask yourself if you have enough work for a full-time employee. Could you get along with a part-time worker, a student or a free lancer?
2. Establish a profile of the type of person you want to hire.
3. Interview carefully. If you are hiring a full-time employee, make a contract that fully outlines the duties of that employee. Be upfront about the salary, about the prospects and about your own prospects. Say what you expect and encourage an honest response.

4. Do not hire someone because you need company during the day.
5. Request pertinent information from your provincial Department of Labour and from Revenue Canada. There are forms to fill out; fill them out properly. Find out about minimum wage, vacation time, sick leave, etc. By law you must adhere to certain standards.
6. Be selective. The current economic situation has resulted in a number of excellent people being on the job market. But don't hire a former manager to file. A highly qualified person in a routine job is likely to be bored, and the bored are not usually good employees.
7. Put a probation period into the contract (ninety days is the usual amount of time). If either of you is unhappy, you can call it quits.
8. Pay the going wage for the work to be done.
9. Be a leader. Inspire your employees by example.
10. Hire people you like and can work with. All the skills in the world will not compensate for a bad personal relationship.
11. Don't be afraid to dismiss an employee, but know the law. In most jurisdictions you must give two-weeks notice or pay the employee for two weeks. If it becomes necessary for you to dismiss an employee, do not procrastinate.
12. Do unto others . . .

Chapter 14
Workstyles/Lifestyles

When you go solo you have the opportunity to integrate your lifestyle and workstyle. Whether you are employed at home or in an office, working on your own as the captain of your ship is a different experience than working for others. You are faced with the questions, "How do I want to live?" and "How do I want to work?"

For many years most North Americans have lived and worked within a known structure. From school to workplace, most of our lives have been lived within a specific daily pattern. But the soloist must make his or her own pattern or routine, and in many solo careers, there is no daily pattern because the variety of occupations makes each day a little different.

Fred Bird quit his nine-to-five job because he couldn't tolerate being asked why he wasn't in the office at nine o'clock sharp rather than at nine-fifteen or nine-thirty. One of the authors of this book prefers an eleven-to-seven working day rather than the traditional nine-to-five working day.

Soloists are usually deeply absorbed and excited by their work. They may work different hours than salaried workers, but they often work longer hours.

Janet Rosenstock of Freelance Writing Associates, Inc. is at her desk in the summer at seven-thirty in the morning, eight-thirty in the winter. Sometimes she takes a short afternoon nap, and sometimes she works twelve hours a day because she's lost in her fiction or has a deadline to meet.

Creating a life structure to replace what was known is the first problem the soloist must deal with. William Sutton is disciplined about his work hours. He loves his family as much as his work and works five days a week, ten hours a day and that is absolutely his limit. As long as he disciplines himself, there is no problem with a well-integrated life.

Marlys Carruthers and her friends from Happy Cookers Publishing Ltd. spend two days per week on their company and the rest of the time on their other responsibilities. They may take tasks away from their meetings to do on other days, and they may schedule travelling into their routine. They, like Bill Sutton, integrate life and work easily through discipline.

While the salaried employee is rushing back to the office at noon hour, Lynn Hubacheck and Nathan Zavier might be having a leisurely lunch discussing creative ideas for new business ventures. Cathy Deuber might be relaxing with a friend. The pets she is responsible for do not require her services till six; so she can spend some time networking.

It is essential for the soloist to learn to pace himself or herself. The soloist must learn to take off time when the time is available. By the same token, work that is not done at one time can usually be done at another. But self-discipline is essential.

Many entrepreneurs enjoy returning to what might be called "the whole job." But doing the whole job requires planning and scheduling so that you have variety in a day's work. You will be involved in sales, advertising, public relations, accounting, developing contacts, networking and keeping the office maintained. As a soloist you are in a situation that calls upon all your skills and demands that you learn new ones.

But all soloists discover the "seasons" of their work. There are times when you will be so busy you do not know what to do, but there will be slow periods as well. It's during the slow periods that the soloist must learn to relax and take advantage of leisure time. You may have to learn to take winter vacations because you are busiest in the summer; you may have to learn to work on holidays and make your own new holidays. Christmas in August? Well, if you are happy, why not?

Successful integration of workstyle and lifestyle depends on many factors. It depends on the kind of business you have, on the demands of that business, on whether or not you have a family, on your own personality and on your ability to relax as well as discipline yourself.

Working at home can be a terrible problem for the individual who can't stand to be alone. There is *no noise* and that will drive a social creature mad. Such an individual is well advised to acquire a partner or find someone to communicate with on a regular basis.

On the other hand, there are many solitary soloists who truly enjoy being alone and whose work, in fact, demands peace and quiet.

The soloist should be aware of the problem of isolation. Isolation is quite different from the solitude of the working day (if solitude is required). It is advisable for the soloist to find a club, or sport or some other activity that will keep him or her from becoming socially isolated.

Mental health, physical well being and enthusiasm are important to success. The soloist must learn to take care of his or her needs.

The ability to relax is essential to creativity, and your company depends on your creativity. The greatest danger for the soloist is burnout and other stress-related disorders. When you are your own boss and love every aspect of your work, it is hard to play. But play is important to both physical and mental health.

As a soloist, you will work in your own way. There is far more integration between your personality and your workstyle than ever existed before. When you worked in an office, you tidied up your desk at ten to five. All the papers that were put in the "in" basket in the morning were in the "out" basket when you left. Pencils were put back in their containers, correspondence in their appropriate files, and the blotter was once again visible. This is a routine you learned in elementary school, and you went from chiding teacher to chiding office manager. If you worked in a factory, the routine was similiar. Your work station was tidied before you left.

The daily process of putting work away and clearing the desk or work unit may be your style, but if it isn't, no one will chide when you are a soloist. You are suddenly in a classroom without a teacher. Some people use what is called "the vertical filing system." Incoming materials are stacked up. One of the most effective entrepreneurs in publishing is Nat Wartels of Crown Publishers, Inc. His desk is a legend. In fact he has two desks—one just for the overflow. If you are the type of a soloist who thrives in confusion, you no longer have to fight it.

Of course, not every soloist thrives in clutter. If you require neatness, be neat. In short, your personality will no longer be subjected to others. If you are messy but efficient, you don't have to make excuses.

William Sutton starts every morning with his "to do" paperwork. He doesn't leave his office till it is completed, and his desk is clear. For Sutton, there is so much to do that anything less than an organized and disciplined approach to the daily workload would fail. But organization also suits his personality.

Some people cannot organize their minds and their scraps of paper too. Other cannot organize their minds without organizing their scraps of paper. As a soloist you should be interested in one thing and one thing only—getting the job done effectively, efficiently and profitably. Your way of dealing with paperwork and pressure can be the way that is best for your personality.

Setting Your Own Hours

There are soloists who run profitable companies working four hours a day, and others who work constantly. A great deal depends on the nature of your business. If you are in retail, you have to maintain certain shopping hours. But you may have an employee that fills in for you during certain hours. If you offer a service, you work at the hours you are contracted to work. If you are performing a service that can be done on your own time, you choose the time. It is likely that you will have a deadline. It doesn't matter if you take off four hours on a Wednesday because you know how long the job will take and you know you can make up the time on Tuesday night. Some soloists are morning people and prefer working from six a.m. to one p.m. Others are night people and find it easier to work from late afternoon into the night.

Dianne Shore makes it a point to be home at five or six p.m. because she enjoys the man she lives with and adores her dogs.

Laurie Greenwood of Greenwood's Books works long hours along with her sister and brother, but they allow each other personal time off.

Lynn Hubacheck and Nathan Zavier can't tolerate routine and boredom; thus they are committed to variety and a multiplicity of different types of assignments. They work at odd hours and relax while others are working.

Priorities

Establishing priorities is an absolute essential for the soloist. When you work for someone else, the priorities are established for you. "Jones, get on this. It's important!"

When you work for yourself, you establish the priorities. If you become preoccupied with day-to-day phone calls, letters, filing and other routine matters, you may find yourself without the time to make sales calls. You know you are in trouble when low priority letters are diligently answered, but you don't have time to collect the money that is owed you. Many small firms have gone bankrupt because the soloists who ran them became overly involved in "busy work." It is said that there is an 80–20 ratio: 80 per cent of your revenue will come from 20 per cent of your accounts. If this is true of your business, you have to apportion your time accordingly. Your accounts have to be mentally divided into large, small and those that have growth potential. You work hardest on the accounts that pay, next hardest on the ones that have growth potential, and you devote the least amount of time to small stagnant accounts. (This is not to suggest you ignore them, they're clients too. But it's a matter of priority.)

As a soloist you no longer have to work closely with people you do not get along with. An old saying goes, "God gave us our relatives, thank heaven we can choose our own friends." The soloist, with rare exception, can choose his or her working relationships. For Fred Bird the right to say "no" is one of the advantages he finds in soloing.

> It hasn't happened often, thank God. There's a couple of times when clients got me in such a way that I will never do work for them again.
>
> Once I was doing a shoot, and this guy looked in my refrigerator and saw a competitive product. He became uptight and said he was going to his car for a minute. He said that when he returned he wanted to see that product in my garbage can.
>
> I told him that when he got into his car, he should keep on going because it wasn't going to happen. No account is going to tell me how to run my life.
>
> I felt bad about that. I don't want to be known as a bad guy.

Should you feel as Fred Bird did, you don't have to continue working with the account. But there are rules to follow when you turn away an account. The first one is to fulfill your contract (or legal obligations) with the same careful work that you would have done had you liked the person. The next is never to accept work from this person again, and the third is to avoid bad mouthing them. You may not have liked the individual or his or her way of doing business, but you will want to stand clear of fall-out. Do your job. Fill your legal responsibilities, and put distance between yourself and your irritation.

Time

Time for most soloists is a precious commodity. For the salaried employee, time can be bought. The salaried employee has a certain number of hours to do a specific task. If the task is not completed, the employee is seen to be slack or he is judged to be overworked. In the latter case, support staff can be hired.

For the soloist, the option of hiring additional staff is not always available. How the soloist deals with time can determine the success or failure of the venture.

Joanna Campion's business is only two years old, and she has already run out of spare time during the day. She has had to be ruthless in the establishment of her priorities. Many of the routine tasks have been delegated to staff. Joanna says she does three things for her company: "That which no one can do, that which makes the company money, and only what I have to do."

When Walter Schroeder began his firm, eating out was the first outside expense to be eliminated. His funds were committed to Dominion Bond Rating Ltd. Today, after seven years, Walter and his wife seldom eat at home; there isn't enough time.

Sam Blyth began his company in October 1977. In the beginning most of his time was spent on building and creating the business. Besides the Show Train and *The Mississippi Belle*, Sam conducts several cross-country bicycle tours in France and also owns an interest in two French language schools in France and three schools that specialize in marine biology.

Sam's greatest challenge is coming up with new ideas, and he does that well. His greatest frustration is not having enough time to implement his ideas. His tour business is on a solid footing, and he has built a comfortable lifestyle for himself. "My business has made me free," he says. At the moment, he does not want to put extra hours into implementing his new ideas. "If I did, I would become a full-time administrator. I don't want that."

Sam has the frustration that comes from not implementing his new ideas and the discipline to know what would happen if he did. He has curtailed himself in order to maintain his business at its present size so he can have the time to enjoy life a little.

Brian Brittain of Tranquility Tanks would also like to spend more time away from his company but hasn't found a way to do so yet. When he is around, there is more business. He would like to find a way to "be there," without actually "being there."

William Sutton will work no more than nine or ten hours a day, five days a week. He says he is not a workaholic, but wants to get the job done. As he says, "No bullshit, just get down to it." The nine to ten hours each day devoted to business are "concentrated" time. There is no time to stare at walls. There is only time to do the job. He enjoys his home and family and does not take work home.

Time pressures in Sutton's business are always intense. Every account wants their work done "yesterday." Time off for Sutton becomes extremely important. His evenings and weekends are a time for regeneration.

Good Times/Bad Times

Soloists, especially in the beginning, learn to live with good times and bad times. Living with the ups and downs of your business will require both an ability to enjoy success and an ability to endure failure. Fred Bird enjoys the social side of success.

> You gotta have fun. When a big job comes into the studio, I'll take everybody to lunch. There's always a party in the studio whenever we finish shooting an issue of *Canadian Living*. You would think we are all nuts. Sometimes guys who used to work for me will drop by. They're in business now for themselves, and they're all doing well. We'll crack open a bottle of champagne or open a bottle of wine and yahoo it up.
>
> Now that I'm getting a bit older, I've decided to slow down a bit. Everytime a big job comes in, I can't go out and get roaring drunk. I had a big job recently of putting together an annual report for a company. For two weeks, I was flying

around the country with my client. By the time we returned to Toronto, we were friends, and along with our wives, go out to dinner occasionally. If I'm not having fun, then my work becomes a job.

Kelly LaBrash would like the story that was told by one of Thomas Edison's assistants. Whenever Edison completed an invention he would jump up and down, doing a kind of Zulu war dance, swearing something awful. His staff would crowd around him and Edison would show his new invention, explaining it to the pattern maker, telling everyone what to do about it.

> When we first started in the uniformed guard business, I would look with envy at the pay my employees were getting. They would be paid before me. In the beginning, if I was lucky, I would be taking home maybe fifty dollars per week. That's less than half of what the guards were making.
>
> When the business finally turned into the black, we certainly celebrated. Sometimes we probably celebrated too much. We were feeling good, we had worked hard, and we survived.

On the other hand, Walter Schroeder does not make a big deal out of celebrating successes, being more philosophical or deriving pleasure from the work itself.

> I'm reluctant to celebrate my successes. I'm afraid that it would be a double whammy the other way. If we do a good job, we know it. If we question whether or not we did a good job, then there's reason to be concerned.

William Sutton feels the same way.

> Maybe I'm still a worrier. I do the George Foster policy, and I feel fine. Then I tell myself that was yesterday, what am I going to do today?
>
> I was very much influenced by a piece I read by Buckminster Fuller. He felt that our society was too much influenced by achieving goals. There was that initial elation at the achievement but two days later who cared. I adopted that attitude. The name of the game is to do what you like to do everyday. Enjoy what you are doing, and all your goals will happen: the money, the fame, the achievement. If you only live

> for the achievement, your life will be empty. If you are unhappy at what you are doing, achieving your goals will not make you happy.

Dealing with the down periods requires an ability to persevere. Depression and fear are sometimes part of the solo experience. There is no carefree road to success and wealth. Judy Snyder of Derbles Bookstore explains how she copes:

> When I'm feeling down, I try to be by myself. I'll go home and spend some time with myself figuring out rational solutions to my problems. I've been known to tie one on during these periods. I don't like to inflict my down mood on others if I can help it. Mostly, I just try to work out the problem, work through it, and then I can get back on top.
>
> I don't think I'm the kind of person who could go through a bankruptcy. It would just about kill me. I would feel terribly deflated and that I had wasted two, three or five years. Then my logical self would take over. It would point out how much fun I had and how much I had learned. I would be okay then.

William Sutton honestly shares his personal feelings about the worry and fear involved in going solo. Again, the name of the game is to walk through the fear, and cope with worry in an intelligent manner.

> My wife commented to a friend that my greatest change was that I stopped being a worrier. I still worry now, but a lot less than when I worked at my last job.
>
> I would talk to myself and say that worry doesn't help. I know what I am doing, and I'm good at it. There is lots of activity, and I'm not in danger of going bankrupt. Then I say to myself "fine" and go home and go to sleep. But sometimes, maybe at three in the morning, I'll suddenly wake up and say, "Holy shit, what if this or that happens?"
>
> This doesn't happen to me now as much as it used to. Occasionally I can let myself get myself down. That is probably the single biggest problem people have. For me now, it is not what I do or when I do it, but how forceful I am while doing it, the confidence I feel in myself. My attitude is work hard, and it will work out.

Len Kubas of Kubas Research Consultants had his share of worries and fears as well.

> I had so many misgivings in the first year. I was taking some projects on which not only did I have to research, I had to also do the selling. I had some part-time students in my office who would work hard while I was there. As soon as I left, all hell would break loose. I couldn't supervise and sell at the same time. I was also troubled by money problems.
>
> At times like that I would just work harder. When you lose sight of your goal, you redouble your effort. I've always been a hard worker. Then and even now I work about one hundred hours per week. The only way I can get through a problem is just by working.

Many soloists look back on their beginning years and laugh about their poverty. Sam Blyth's tour business now grosses five million dollars a year, and yet when he started he didn't know if he had enough money for the morning paper. He didn't even bother to check his pockets. Andrew Crosbie and Angus McKay share their first three years:

> The first three years were the toughest. All the money we had and whatever we could borrow from banks and the family went into the business. We gave up eating at restaurants and, once in a while, eating all together. We stopped buying new clothes, taking vacations, and occasionally we would just work around the clock to bring in a few dollars. But hell, we were doing it for a reason. We didn't like it, but if we got the job done, we could relax and enjoy ourselves later.

Today Fred Bird has the ability to travel south whenever he wants to, and he has a personal, spendable income far in excess of top photographers who still work for others in large corporations.

> To hell with tax advantages, I didn't take a salary out of my business for the first year because there wasn't enough money. Fortunately my wife was working at the time, and was able to support me for that first year. The second year, I was able to take an occasional draw from the company.
>
> We had to give up eating out and travelling south. I had to make up my mind that I wanted this little number to go. I just

> said to myself . . . everything else has got to sit for a while. The business comes first.

Personal Development

The life of the soloist is a life of learning, and learning pays dividends in both the personal sense and for your business or corporation. The soloist should never become too busy to spend time acquiring information and new skills.

Eunice Webster spends the first forty-five minutes of every day on personal development. Her company is devoted to personal development, and the company starts with her own belief in continued learning. Some mornings she is learning speed-reading, at other times she is listening to tapes on how to reach goals through planning, or how to break the worry habit.

Nathan Zavier and Lynn Hubacheck feel it's essential to take courses. They enjoy them. Nathan has just finished taking a course at Ryerson on hotel and resort management because he'd love a share of the tourist market. Lynn, on the other hand, is concerned about learning as much as she can about accounting, money and investments.

Michael Gowling quit school at sixteen and has returned at thirty. He needs to know more about business even though he is extremely successful.

> I have to go back and study business now that I'm on my own. I have to know bookkeeping and accounting and balance sheets. When I was in high school the people who studied business were the creeps. I was one of the creative ones with the cameras and art equipment. The biggest problem with people starting out in business today is they don't have business knowledge. You have to know bookkeeping, and you have to have a sense of accounting. You have to be able to set up a business plan. If you can go out and sell a product to a corporation, you can certainly go out and sell yourself to a banker. You've got to be able to talk the banker's language which means you have to have a financial statement and a projected cash flow. If I want to take a good picture I have to know how to operate a camera. In order to get money out of the bank, I have to know where the levers are.
>
> I know a lot of people who get turned down by the banks.

> They say, 'The bank didn't buy my idea, they didn't think my idea would work.' That isn't it at all. The bank simply didn't have faith that the person had the managerial ability to do it. That is why you have to take the time to learn it.

Whatever you choose to study, learn enough so that you have a working knowledge of the subject. Talent is the sum total of a person's knowledge and experience, plus the ability to put that knowledge and experience to use.

None of the soloists interviewed felt they knew enough about business. Even Walter Schroeder who rates some of the largest corporations in the country spends time learning. Nancy Thomson is constantly updating and refining her knowledge.

Take time to expand your knowledge. Read, take courses, share your experiences with others.

Allow time in your day for personal development. Part of personal development is to acquire what is known as vision. Vision is more than a pleasant daydream; it is your plan for the future. Knowing where you want to go and how you want to live pays off. Eunice Webster knows the value of dreams.

> Dreams are a creative process. The ability to dream about possibilities is essential. From my dreams I pick certain elements and that helps me to select the things I want to do.
>
> Many times when I'm sitting here in the basement, I'm painting mental pictures. It keeps me going. When I'm here in my office with the concrete walls, the broken bike and the cat's litter box, I'm on the phone talking to someone about success. While I'm on the phone, I'm not sitting in the basement in my mind, I'm in one of the most gorgeous offices you've ever seen in your life. I've laughed when I got off the phone. 'Wow, this isn't where I was a minute ago.' Dreams are important. I don't think you could have a business of your own without those kinds of dreams.

For most soloists, their daydreams become their vision, and their visions become goals. They are willing to work because they know where they want to go and what they want to be able to do.

As a soloist, workstyle and lifestyle are integrated. Both are manifestations of the individual's personality.

Chapter 15

In Conclusion

Ed Polanski has come a long way since he was a kid out of school installing cables in the town of Athabasca. Today he is one of the television cable industry's leading spokesmen. Ed is known by the button he wears on his lapel. It reads: **Up Your Entrepreneurship**!

In a speech delivered to the Canadian Cable Association in June 1982, Ed spoke on this theme, saying that he lives by the principle that "when the economy goes down, entrepreneurship must go up." He suggests that entrepreneurship will be "the main survival mechanism" of our economy in the 1980s. For Ed, going solo is the only answer.

The economy is in dire straits, and many traditional areas are breaking down. In order to survive, according to Ed:

> We need again to be aggressive in dealing with a risky and hazardous market place—to win a new place at the dawning. To know that our future CEO's (Chief Executive Officers) will have to be hard-nosed entrepreneurs who will establish separate "new venture" companies (and) exploit new business opportunities.

Those who are employed by large corporations are fighting an increasingly difficult foe. Every day brings economic doom and gloom and more news of the latest economic casualties. Bankruptcies are occurring faster than in the Great Depression, and large corporations are deeply in debt to the banks. The employees of many firms are agreeing to take pay cuts; the government is taking steps to hold the line with its employees; inflation remains high; managers with years of experience and seniority are being laid off.

Many large corporations have moved to developing countries or use less expensive labour from other countries, and this has resulted in massive layoffs in North America. We, in Canada, face a specific challenge. A smaller percentage of the population controls the wealth of this nation than in any other country in the industrialized world, because so few Canadians are the owners of their own companies. Concentration of wealth and power lead to disaster. When a giant falls, he falls over a large area.

No industry better illustrates the danger inherent in concentration than the automobile industry in which North Americans have currently lost 30 per cent of the market. Added to dislocations caused by this factor is the dislocation of the technological revolution which is well underway.

New companies must be created for the new technology. New ideas will sell, and it is up to you to think of them and make them happen through your own work. Few soloists interviewed had it easy. Virtually all of them had to work long, hard hours to achieve success. Some have become wealthy, and most feel far more secure financially than those who work for others. Best of all, the majority of the soloists live a life of freedom, self-fulfillment and independence, of satisfaction and potency due to their own direct efforts.

Going solo is no guarantee of an easy life, but working for someone else is a guarantee of limited options. As a soloist your working conditions will sometimes be difficult, and it may take many years to see the fruits of your labour. But going solo will provide you with a freer life, one filled with more opportunities than you can presently imagine. You will be able to establish a business that reflects your own personality, and you will be able to ride the waves of the fluctuating economy.

Go solo. You have nothing to lose but your chains.

Appendix
Meet the Soloists

Dennis Adair and Janet Rosenstock, *Freelance Writing Associates, Inc.* Dennis and Janet have been a writing team and partnership since 1974, only recently incorporating. They started writing educational and corporate copy and have since moved on to best-selling fiction.

Mario Barocchi, *Art World 700 Ltd.* Mario began his solo career at the age of sixteen on the streets of Milan, buying and selling paintings. Moving to Toronto, he opened a shop and has since become recognized internationally for his expertise in art and antiques.

Fred Bird, *Fred Bird and Associates.* Fred has been going solo as a photographer since the early 1970s, first in partnership and later by himself. He is probably Canada's leading food and travel photographer. He recently purchased a video-cassette camera, has taken a few courses, and soon will be making his own films.

Sam Blyth, *Blyth and Company.* In 1977, at the age of 22, Sam began his company specializing in personal tours. He has organized the Shaw Festival on a train across Canada and has delighted and entertained thousands on a riverboat down the Mississippi. If you choose to go mountain climbing in Nepal, Sam just may escort you and your party there personally.

Brian Brittain, *Tranquility Tanks.* Brian specializes in the relief of stress, and to that end, he and a partner opened Tranquility Tanks in 1980. For a moderate fee, you can relax peacefully in a salt-water solution, warmed to your body's temperature. If you ask for it, you can have music piped into the tank.

Joanna Campion, *Campion Language Studies.* Joanna began her successful mail-order language studies just as a nation-wide postal strike hit the country in 1980. It took her six weeks to discover that her belief that the market was there was right. There has been wide acceptance of her courses.

Cathy Deuber, *Home Minders.* Cathy purchased her company in 1980 and has built it up to the point that she is now able to seriously consider selling franchises to others who want a secure life watching other people's homes.

Doug Dunbar, *College Copy Shop.* Doug opened his doors for the first time in 1968 to a line-up of people. He now owns three locations in

Toronto, and has financed two other shops which bear the same name in Edmonton and Kingston.

Mary I. Duncan, *Document Examination and Forgery Detection.* Mary has been working as a full-time document examiner and forgery detector since the middle 1960s. She is regarded by the courts of Ontario as a bona fide "expert."

Charlotte Fielden, *Free Lancer.* Charlotte is a soloist who has always gone her own way, doing best what she enjoys most. She has published plays and books, is a minister of the Spiritualist Church, teaches yoga, and has been a film maker.

Michael Gowling, *Michael Gowling Productions.* At the age of sixteen Michael ran away from his home in Hamilton, Ontario. He has been going solo ever since. Now in his early thirties, Michael specializes in the production of non-broadcast, industrial films. His soloing has taken him all over the world.

Audrey Grant, *The Toronto Bridge Club.* Audrey owns one of Toronto's most successful bridge clubs. She has created an excellent setting for competitive to novice-level bridge. In business since 1980, she has her entire family working with her.

Brad, Gail and Laurie Greenwood, *Greenwood's Books.* These three siblings started their bookstore in Edmonton in 1979. All are in their twenties, and their energy and enthusiasm is reflected in the vitality of their store.

Sharon James, *Sharon's Catering Service.* Sharon joined the ranks of soloists in 1981. The business got off to a shaky start, but fortunately the word of mouth about her cooking is making her a sensation in Toronto.

Joyce Krusky, Lynn McLaughlin, and Marlys Carruthers, *Happy Cookers Publishing Ltd.* Joyce, Lynn and Marlys are three Alberta friends (and housewives) who love to cook. They decided to write, publish and distribute their own cookbook. At last count, *Good to the Last Bite* has sold over 40,000 copies.

Len Kubas, *Kubas Research Consultants* and *Retail Marketing Communications.* At the age of forty, Len felt it was time to see if he could become a success on his own. He quit his job, bought a word-processor, installed it in his basement, and has not looked back since. Len has been going solo since 1977.

Kelly LaBrash, *Canadian Protection Services Ltd.* A soloist since 1967, Kelly does not look at all like Sam Spade or James Rockford, but he does run Canada's largest investigation and security agency. At times his company employs over a thousand people. He recently sold his company to the Argus Corporation, which has kept him on as president.

Joan Lavers, *What's Cooking?* Joan started her retail kitchen shop in 1978. This is one of the few retail shops in the Cabbagetown section of Toronto to make money in the past few years. Joan maintains that much of her success is attributable to avoiding bank loans.

Ed Polanski, *QCTV.* Ed started his cable television company in 1959 in the town of Athabasca, Alberta. From a base of 6,000 subscribers, he has built up a network of over ten stations with almost 150,000 subscribers in Alberta and British Columbia.

George Prokos, *Public Relations Board of Canada.* George has been going solo as a public relations consultant, starting in 1969 at the age of forty-five. The Public Relations Board of Canada is a big name for a small business.

Walter J. Schroeder, *Dominion Bond Rating Service Ltd.* Walter created his company in 1977, after serving a valuable apprenticeship on Bay Street. He enjoys being a "referee" on the bond market, and having a major say on companies hundreds of times larger than his own.

Dianne Shore, *Dianne Shore, Interior Planners Ltd.* In 1965, at the age of twenty-five, Dianne began her company at home. She is now a major real estate owner in downtown Toronto.

Sandy Simpson, *The S.L. Simpson Gallery.* Sandy opened her art gallery at the age of twenty-two, renting a house that had living accommodations and space for her "dream" gallery. She now actively displays the work of emerging talent, and is an internationally respected art dealer.

Art Smolensky, *The Lens 'n' Shutter.* Art opened his first camera shop in 1970, almost around the corner from his home in the Kitsilano section of Vancouver. He has built the one store into a small chain and thriving mail-order business.

Judy Snyder, *Derbles Bookstore.* Judy fought the economy as long as she could, but there just wasn't a place for her bookstore in downtown Toronto.

William J. Sutton, *Special Risk Insurance, Inc.* Ten days after he was fired as executive vice-president for a large insurance company, William started his own agency. Specializing in sports insurance, he has branched out into many new and lucrative aspects of underwriting and brokering.

Nancy Thomson, *Nancy Thomson/Investing for Women.* Nancy offers investment courses for women throughout the country. Beginning alone in 1978, she now has offices in thirteen cities and employs over fifty individuals.

Eunice Webster, *Apex Associates*. Originally from California, Eunice moved to Toronto when her daughter was accepted into the National Ballet School. She began her business in her basement in 1980. Apex Associates is dedicated to helping individuals reach their life goals.

Mikki West, *Pamper Yourself*. Mikki was the moving force behind this co-operative venture which began in 1978. Mikki has been successfully building Pamper Yourself into a complete beauty service centre under one roof.

Michael G. Woods, *Accountant*. After three years as a C.A. with a large firm, Michael decided to go solo. He has had his own company since 1976.

Nathan Zavier and Lynn Hubacheck, *Go Fer Enterprises*. Founded in 1979, Go Fer Enterprises caters to any legal request for their services. If someone has neither the time nor the knowledge of how to do virtually anything, Lynn and Nathan will do it (or find someone who will).

Bibliography

A considerable number of books were used as background for this work. Some of them were terrible, while others merely covered isolated points. The bulk of the information came directly from the soloists interviewed. Nevertheless, several books were found to be extremely valuable for their perspective, others for their concrete suggestions. A partial list of the books we found most valuable follows.

General

The Third Wave, Alvin Toffler (William Morrow & Co, N.Y., 1980). This is the definitive book on the future. It is also the definitive book on today.

Small is Beautiful, E.F. Schumacher (Sphere Books, London, 1973). This could become the "bible" for small business.

How to Turn Your Ideas Into a Million Dollars, Don Kracke (Mentor Books, N.Y., 1979). Written by the inventor of "Rickie, Tickie, Stickies," this book tells the inside story of his invention and a variety of seemingly "off the wall" ideas that turned into millions, including the story of Gary Dahl and the Pet Rock.

How to Become Financially Successful Owning Your Own Business, Albert J. Lowry (Simon & Schuster, N.Y., 1981). After building up his fortune in real estate, Lowry has tackled owning a business. With his heavy cash reserves, Lowry has become an advocate of "buying" an existing business, rather than starting one's own.

The Magic of Thinking Big, David J. Schwartz (Simon & Schuster, N.Y., 1981). This little book has been around since 1959, and for good reason. It is the best pep talk in print.

How to Beat the Salary Trap, Richard K. Rifenbark (Avon Books, N.Y., 1979). An excellent book which offers a variety of ideas on how to make money while working for the corporation.

The Entrepreneur's Guide, Deaver Brown (Ballantine Books, N.Y., 1981). Brown is the inventor of the "Umbroller," the folding baby stroller. This is an excellent first-person account of going solo.

Edison: The Man Who Made the Future, Ronald W. Clarke (Putnam, N.Y., 1977). If you think you have crazy ideas that will never work, read this brilliant biography of the world's greatest inventor and businessman.

Specific

It's Your Money, J. Christopher Snyder and Brian E. Anderson (Methuen, Toronto, 1982). This fine book, now in its third edition, explains clearly and succinctly just what money is all about.

The New Canadian Tax and Investment Guide, Henry B. Zimmer (Hurtig, Edmonton, 1981). This book is designed solely for the well-paid business person and executive, hence no soloist should be without it. The cost of the book is more than made up by the suggested tax savings.

You Can Negotiate Anything, Herb Cohen (Bantam Books, N.Y., 1982). The best book on the market. Cohen advocates the "win/win" type of negotiating. His examples range from the multi-billion-dollar deal to successfully haggling at a department store for the demonstrator model.

How to Get Control of Your Time and Your Life, Alan Lakein (Signet, N.Y., 1974). An invaluable source on how to "priorize" your time.

The Godfather, Mario Puzo (Putnam, N.Y., 1969). There is no better book on the dynamics of the family business, and the type of problems it can encounter. Do not—Repeat *do not*—read this book for advice on how to get paid.